PRESCRIPTIONS FOR PURPOSE

Medicine, Choices, and the Impact of Compassionate Care

WILFRED NJAH, MD

ACTION WEALTH PUBLISHING
www.ActionWealthPublishing.com

Kemp House
152 -160 City Road
London, EC1V 2NX
United Kingdom

ISBN: 978-1-917451-25-3
Published by Action Wealth Publishing and Wilfred Njah
Printed in the United States

*I dedicate this book to my parents, Beatrice and Joseph-Lawrence Njah, and my mentors,
Joseph and Akwi Fonbah, and Dr. Brian Sims.*

I also dedicate it to my beloved Glory, Tita, Nahyahkah Mah-Kah, Njong-Timah, and all the children of the Kids of Tomorrow Foundation orphanage
(www.KOT-foundation.org)

CONTENTS

ACKNOWLEDGMENTS

Thank you, Mom and Dad, for the solid foundation you provided me with. I view the world through the lessons you taught me. To my beloved wife, Mrs. Glory Njah: Your support has made me more tenacious. Tita, Nahyahkah Mah, and Njong-Timah: thank you for motivating me. I look forward to the day you tell your own stories.

Mr. Joseph and Mrs. Akwi Fonbah, you supported my journey through your nephew, Dr. Hope, and imparted invaluable wisdom. Dr. Brian Sims, thank you for your guidance and mentorship; you encouraged me to mentor others, and I haven't stopped since.

Dr. Wilfred Ngwa and Dr. Lydia Asana, thank you for the invaluable lessons I learned during my Harvard Global Health Catalyst fellowship. Mr. Geoffrey Semaganda, your rigorous teachings on personal development have made this book possible.

I am forever grateful to my siblings for your prayers and support.

INTRODUCTION

I have dedicated my life to the noble profession of medicine. As a doctor, I have witnessed the transformative power of compassionate care, healed physical ailments, and positively influenced all aspects of life.

Writing has always been my refuge, a therapeutic release I indulge in during my spare time. I believe that books, like the human body, are a wealth of knowledge waiting to be discovered. They document our collective experiences and serve as an influential platform to captivate audiences, build trust, and even galvanize action toward noble causes like philanthropy and business innovation.

My journey so far has been a cocktail of victories and adversities. It is a narrative filled with moments of joy and sorrow, triumphs and trials, each chapter a testament to the resilience of the human spirit. I sincerely hope that as you read my story, you'll find a connection, a shared experience, or an emotion that resonates with you.

I want to inspire you to keep striving and pushing the boundaries of what is possible. Every challenge we face holds a lesson, a nugget of wisdom to be unearthed. My earnest desire is that through my experiences, you'll find the courage to keep flourishing, to keep accomplishing, and above all, to keep caring.

Before we begin, I would like to share a poem I wrote:

I Stand! However:

Wherever I am, as I go, there I stand!

With the past and present side by side

To look and learn which one to take

But must go forward every which way

Wherever I go, I take them with me

Grannies, uncles, siblings, and their multitude.

Wherever I am, I hold the flame, best as I understand.

With callused hands and an ocean behind

Though confident, but with a bit of trembling

I take daring steps, then another as I go

Building the team daily and taking them along with me

Wherever I go, mentors and mentees go with gratitude...

CHAPTER ONE

EARLY STEPPING STONES

I was born into the loving embrace of my parents, Beatrice and Joseph-Lawrence, in the serene city of Bamenda in the Northwest Province of Cameroon. I am the second amongst a brood of six biological offspring, a position that came with its unique blend of responsibilities and privileges. Nevertheless, the concept of family in our household extended far beyond the confines of biological ties. Our parents' hearts had enough room to hold many more children, and they did this per the traditions of our Moghamo culture.

In Moghamo culture and numerous other cultures worldwide, newlyweds are often responsible for nurturing and raising a younger sibling or relative. While seemingly generous, this practice is deeply rooted in the belief that it bestows blessings upon the couple, paving the way for them to have their children.

This notion of adoption preceding childbearing is not uncommon. It is a thread woven through the fabric of many cultures; in ours, it is the norm rather than the exception. The age-old African adage, "It takes a village to raise a child," found a true home in our family, with each member playing a role in shaping the lives and destinies of the others.

Our parents, deeply devout Christians, ran a relatively disciplined household. My mother, a businesswoman who devoted her time and energy to her entrepreneurial ventures, was the quintessential matriarch, balancing work and family with admirable finesse. On the other hand, my father was a chief registrar at the Court of First Instance, a trial court of primary jurisdiction. He instilled the importance of justice, integrity, and hard work.

As children, we were privileged to attend some of our province's most prestigious boarding schools, a testament to our parents' commitment to our education. Economically, we hovered comfortably in the middle class, but our rich values and principles genuinely defined us. Our upbringing centered on the pillars of love for God and love for each other, values that remain deeply ingrained in us today.

Learning Business Through My Parents

My upbringing was deeply influenced by my parents' unique roles and teachings. My father, a humble and intelligent man, instilled in me the keys to success, not through the lens of accomplishments but through understanding and avoiding failures and seeking the lessons underlying them. His approach broke conventional norms in our culture, where discussions about elders' shortcomings are shunned.

However, my father encouraged open dialogue, allowing me to brainstorm ways to overcome potential challenges. Our relationship was not limited to the traditional father-son bond but extended to a friendship fostered during our shared television viewing experiences.

On the other hand, my relationship with my mother was also unique and multi-layered. She worked diligently six days a week as a full-time businesswoman, maintaining a rigorous eight-hour work shift. Simultaneously, she held the position of counselor in the village government.

I had a dual role regarding my mother as her son and as an apprentice. This dynamic presented its challenges, as she was a no-nonsense boss requiring discipline and dedication. As I navigate and reflect on my youth and memories, I have come to appreciate my mother's remarkable ability to effectively balance her roles as both a mother and a boss. Her teachings were integral in shaping my understanding of work ethics and the importance of maintaining a balanced life.

Early Desires of a Medical Career

My mother often recounted stories from my childhood, including my peculiar obsession with rabbits. Not for their fluffy tails or playful nature but as potential 'patients' for my pretend surgeries. From a very young age, medicine was not just a fascination but a deeply ingrained passion.

During family gatherings, when we would share our dreams and aspirations, I vividly remember announcing my grand plans to my siblings. I dreamt of becoming a physician, not just any, but one who owned a hospital - a sanctuary where I could amass the ill and provide them with the care they needed.

Our family, like any other, wasn't immune to health adversities. I bore witness to the crippling effects of asthma that tormented my brother and father. Their episodes were so severe that I often found myself consumed by fear, fearing the worst. These experiences didn't deter me; they fortified my resolve to pursue a medical career.

My educational journey began in an era without encouragement for critical thinking and questioning. The educational system seemed to be more of a rigid structure rather than an entity encouraging intellectual curiosity and fostering unique perspectives. Despite these limitations, I held onto my dream of becoming a medical doctor.

My curiosity was ignited during my secondary school years when I dove headfirst into the world of science. The profound contributions of Einstein and Newton fascinated me, piquing my interest and fueling my passion for understanding the mysteries of life. I desired to attend the type of university where Einstein and Newton made their discoveries.

However, the curriculum was not without its flaws. It primarily focused on Western civilization and European history and disregarded the rich tapestry of African society and history. This cultural void seemed inappropriate and was noticeable even to us, the children. Moreover, the teaching methods were one-dimensional, relying heavily on classroom lectures, multiple-choice questions, and essays. There was no emphasis on catering to the individual's unique learning style, which was a significant oversight.

Despite these challenges, my passion for medicine never wavered. It strengthened my resolve to change the status quo, learn, and eventually contribute to the medical field. These early experiences and passions and my dogged determination formed the footholds on my path toward a medical career.

During my high school years, another health crisis struck our family. One of my siblings was diagnosed with pneumonia, a battle that was painful and debilitating. Each health challenge my family faced was a catalyst, further solidifying my aspiration to become a physician.

There was a time when I ascended from one academic level to the next with merits that could barely be considered substantial. This was what we referred to as being "promoted on trial." In this grade and the ones that followed, I dedicated myself entirely, striving to secure a spot among the top ten achievers. Finally, my efforts paid off as I landed the 9th position, with commendable grades in Biology, Chemistry, and Physics. This achievement laid the foundation for my future premedical education.

Just before my departure to America, I experienced a loss that left a profound impact on me. The person whom I was named after, a significant figure in my life, succumbed to lung cancer, despite having never smoked for a day in his life. His passing was a painful reminder of the fragility of life and the importance of health. The memories of him, however, carried with me across the ocean, a bittersweet remembrance of our shared bond.

His presence wasn't confined to my memories alone but seemed to transcend the realm of dreams. In times of difficult decisions, he would appear in my dreams, offering guidance through scriptures, just as he used to when he was alive. His spiritual presence was a testament to our profound connection, even transcending the barriers of life and death.

These experiences and my inherent passion for medicine shaped my early youth and fueled my desire to enter medicine. Each health crisis that my family faced was a step, propelling me further toward my goal of becoming a physician. They taught me the importance of health and care and solidified my commitment to medicine.

Family Background

In my early years, I differed from the thoughtful and composed individual I am today. A fondness marked my childhood for toy cars and soccer cards, with a solid comparison to the baseball cards in American neighborhoods. Between the ages of 8 and 10 years, I had amassed a fascinating collection of these items. Some toy cars were handcrafted by my elder brother, Martin, while others were victors' trophies from local games and friendly wagers. The prized possessions of my collection were soccer cards featuring the legends of the game: Platini, Maradona, and Pelé.

These cards were more than just pieces of cardboard to me; they were symbolic of prestige and recognition. I was known far and wide in our locality as the kid with the finest collection, a cherished recognition. However, preserving this status often led me into contentious situations. The world of card collecting was competitive, and maintaining my standing meant ensuring that the losers in our betting games surrendered their card collections. This practice often led to fights.

Our betting games varied in scale. When the stakes were low, we used cards featuring lesser-known soccer players. However, when the stakes were raised, the cards of esteemed players like Maradona came into play. Eventually, my mischievous exploits caught the attention of my father. Initially, in disbelief, he took time to observe my antics, and fearing the crowd of card collectors and playmates I was dealing with, he shared his findings with my mother.

To divert my energy from these frays, my father suggested that my mother involve me in her business. This marked the beginning of my journey into the world of business. It was a transformative phase that shaped me into who I am today.

Growing up, my father was one of the trailblazers in our community, owning one of the first cars in our vicinity, a Renault 12. This car became a symbol of our family's status, etched in the memories of my childhood friends. Even today, conversations with old companions often revolve around recollections of this vehicle. Though now considered outdated in its simplicity, the car was our pride and joy in those days. We traveled in it on every occasion, with my father skillfully navigating the traffic, sometimes with courtesy, occasionally with impatience.

I remember being captivated by the traffic lights at the General Hospital and City-Chemist roundabouts during our daily commutes. These lights seemed to sense the accumulation of cars, turning green just in time to let them proceed. Their intuition in allowing pedestrians to cross safely was equally intriguing. It reminds me of the innocent times of my youth when almost everything appeared wondrously.

Unfortunately, at 12, political turmoil led to my father's premature retirement and a delay in his pension. Consequently, my mother had to shoulder most of the financial responsibilities. Aware of our circumstances as a child, I contributed to my tuition and allowance. I approached my mother for a loan during my summer break to kick-start a business venture. I took on selling off the stale inventory from her shop. In the process, I managed to generate profit and alleviate some of our financial pressures, and I discovered a budding passion for business.

From Childhood Lessons to Lifelong Success

➤ **Community and Culture Shape Your Foundation**

Growing up in a culture deeply rooted in communal values teaches the significance of shared responsibility and mutual support. The philosophy that "It takes a village to raise a child" reminds you that your success is often built on the contributions of family, mentors, and society. Recognizing this helps you approach life with gratitude and a sense of duty to give back.

➢ Balancing Career and Family Requires Discipline

Watching a mother successfully manage both a business and a household highlights the importance of discipline, organization, and perseverance. Likewise, learning from a father who upholds integrity and justice instills values crucial for professional and personal success. These lessons remind you that balancing career aspirations with family responsibilities is possible with the right mindset and commitment.

➢ Education is a Powerful Tool

Knowledge acquired through education is a gateway to opportunities. Whether your dreams lie in science, medicine, or another field, embracing learning as a lifelong pursuit is key. Additionally, recognizing the gaps in your educational experience, especially in cultural representation and diversity, can inspire you to seek knowledge beyond textbooks and broaden your understanding of the world.

> ## Childhood Interests Can Teach Valuable Life Skills

The simple hobbies and activities you engaged in as a child, such as collecting soccer cards or participating in competitive games, were not just pastimes but early lessons in business, strategy, and negotiation. These experiences helped develop critical thinking, decision-making, and resilience, which proved useful in adulthood.

> ## Entrepreneurship and Initiative Foster Resilience

Financial or family challenges early in life can be difficult, but taking initiative, like starting a small business during summer breaks, helps develop problem-solving skills and independence. These experiences build an entrepreneurial spirit, teaching you how to turn obstacles into opportunities.

> ## Every Experience Contributes to Your Growth

Each phase of life, from childhood to adulthood, presents unique lessons. Whether through family influence, education, personal interests, or financial challenges, these experiences shape your resilience, adaptability, and drive to succeed. Seeing each moment as a step allows you to move forward purposefully and confidently.

Final Thought

Your early experiences serve as a foundation for personal and professional growth. Your lessons about discipline, integrity, entrepreneurship, and lifelong learning are valuable tools that will guide you through life's challenges and opportunities.

Embrace each step as part of your journey toward success, knowing that every experience has contributed to the person you are becoming.

CHAPTER TWO

FINANCIAL HARDSHIP IN AMERICA

In the chronicles of my life, one chapter stands out: a period characterized by a monumental transition and a test of resilience. It was when the winds of change blew me from the familiar terrains of Africa across the vast Atlantic to the land of dreams and opportunities - the United States.

The excursion I embarked on wasn't merely geographical. It was a profound leap into a new world, a shift from the comfort of home to the struggles of a stranger in a foreign land. I found myself in America, the land of the brave and the home of the free yet weighed down by the chains of financial constraints.

The joy of academic success in my school years was bittersweet, tainted by the struggles of making ends meet. This chapter is a testament to those times, a narration of my financial hardships and the resilience that saw me through. It accounts for my journey from Africa to America, a tale of struggle, determination, and the relentless pursuit of dreams.

Family in Africa

In the humble surroundings where I grew up, we were fortunate to have the basics of life but not much after that. Yet, I had an added advantage. I knew the exact extent of my mother's financial capabilities. I often assisted her with her small business and witnessed the daily toils and triumphs she undertook to keep our lives afloat.

As I stepped into the turbulent world of high school, I found myself amidst young boys like me. Our discussions were often heated, passionate, and filled with the zest of youth. We would gather in our usual spot, under the shade of the old mango tree, and discuss the hot topics that buzzed around our neighborhood.

Who had recently landed in trouble and why? Which family had recently paraded with a shiny new car down the narrow streets? What brands adorn us, the young aspirers of society? But above all, our conversations often circled back to the most exciting topic: who had recently traveled?

During those times, our country had a single, overcrowded university where English was the language of instruction. This meant that most English-speaking high school graduates, like us, faced the daunting decision to travel abroad if they wished to pursue careers not offered at the local university.

My heart was set on medicine, a field not offered at the local institution. It seemed a futile pursuit to enroll in a degree that lacked my interest and focus.

So, the decision to travel abroad to pursue my dream of becoming a medical doctor was a no-brainer.

However, traveling to foreign lands and the prospect of affording tuition at a distant university were mountainous challenges for me and my entire family. It was like staring at a towering mountain, with the peak hidden in the clouds, and wondering how we would ever reach the top.

With their unwavering belief in my dreams, my parents made it their life's mission to support me. They worked longer hours, made countless sacrifices, and borrowed money to fund my trip abroad. Their dedication to my cause was nothing short of heroic. They bore the weight of debt, not for themselves, but for the more significant cause of my future.

Venturing overseas can be seen as the beginning of full-fledged adulthood. Now that I'm an adult, it's no longer appropriate to rely on my parents for financial support. Instead, the tables have turned, and it's my responsibility to send money home to help them meet the needs of my brothers and sisters. I took on roles such as a retail assistant and a security officer, allowing me to start saving for my education and contribute to settling the debts my parents had accumulated from funding my expedition to America.

Over time, however, I grew increasingly discontent with my situation.

The job positions I was eligible for offered only bare minimum wages. The lucrative positions were reserved for those who held degrees, a fact made abundantly clear to me as a mere high school graduate. As the months passed, I prayed daily, even fasting, to achieve clarity. The road ahead was daunting.

Yet, the resolve in my parents' eyes fueled my determination to make their sacrifices worthwhile. As I embarked on my journey to foreign shores, I carried their hopes, dreams, and the responsibility of honoring their sacrifices.

Learning Spiritual and Personal Growth

I moved to the United States on the cusp of my twentieth birthday. During my time in Africa, I had always felt that reaching the age of nineteen was a rite of passage towards adulthood, a common perception in a nation where life expectancy was a mere 52 years at that point. However, I soon realized that being twenty is still considered a minor in some parts of America.

In our customs, the family must gather to bestow their blessings before someone goes on a journey like mine. We refer to this as a send-off ceremony. These ceremonies are deeply ingrained in the African lifestyle as a conduit for promoting family welfare.

Such events create an avenue for mending fences between relatives and friends, seen as a crucial step towards ensuring success and harmony.

The prevailing belief is that serenity banishes negativity and ill fortune as one embarks on such voyages. On the eve of my departure, a farewell ritual was conducted for me. On such occasions, family members display utmost reverence for the pecking order. The family's senior members carry out parting ceremonies as they see their ancestors do when one of their own is venturing far away.

The ceremony has abundant food, beverages, heartwarming chats, and tears. Nonetheless, the purpose of such a gathering goes beyond mere social mingling. When goodbyes are said, they are done with the understanding that it may be the final instance. This was true in my case and for some of my dear ones, as future events would later demonstrate.

Mothers and siblings lock their eyes with the departing members and utter solid prayers to provide lifelong protection at some junctures during the ceremony. They invoke divine favor and bestow blessings even for future spouses and offspring yet to arrive.

Immersed in the festivity, I endeavored to etch every detail into my memory: the vibrant hues, the scents, the ringing laughter. This was it! It was no longer a dream but a reality, a moment that would replay throughout my journey. I was accompanied not only by these memories but also by unseen companions whom I believe have been called upon to join me on this journey. However, news of my upcoming trips hadn't permeated the local grapevine yet; such information was disseminated strictly on a need-to-know basis.

This is the usual protocol for such information within our cultural context. My departure to America would be swift, and it would be a while before my absence registered with the local community. When that realization struck, I would inevitably become the subject of neighborhood chatter. As I understood growing up, trust is earned over an entire lifetime. With this hard-earned trust comes the privilege of being given privacy to the personal affairs of those who deem you worthy. Therefore, the secrecy surrounding certain matters stems from a deficiency of this trust token.

The room was teeming with trusted individuals and others who could communicate with our forebears by their unique abilities within our family. Quite a gathering was accompanying me! Having been brought up more in the Christian faith than the African traditional religion, I found myself grappling with a spiritual disconnect. Some speeches during the ceremony featured verses from the Holy Bible, while others invoked ancestors about whom I knew nothing.

Undoubtedly, this ceremony was a grand display of tradition.

The elderly relative who invoked our ancestors for my safe journey is clinging to an archaic practice that predates King James's version of his arrival in our village. Those offering prayers with the rosary and marking their foreheads with the cross sign followed the priest's teachings.

When my father's turn arrived, I knelt before him in a gesture of respect. He stood as my father, symbolizing an enduring lineage of loved ones who preceded him. His voice was steadfast, a tone I hadn't heard him use before, which sent chills down my spine. After expressing that his heart is filled with love for and from his late mother, he sampled some palm wine he had fetched from the village earlier that day. He then sprayed some onto his palm to moisten it and gently rubbed it on my face and head. This act signifies the transmission of strength, love, and all goodness.

Subsequently, he directed me assertively to *get up and go!*

And so, I did; ever since, my days started with rising and shining. As I packed up to leave, their goodbyes echoed around me. It was time for me to head to America. My thoughts were a whirlwind. The images of what I just saw were etched in my mind forever. I vividly remember the uncertainty that clouded me, as I didn't know when I'd be back or if our paths would cross again.

It was a whirlwind trying to comprehend what was happening, where my life was heading, and where I stood between this Christian doctrine and the native African belief system. Interestingly, both traditions caution us against trusting anyone unquestioningly but emphasize spreading love everywhere.

And so, I quietly slipped away from my neighborhood, leaving behind the past and everything that didn't align with my aspirations.

Embarking on the path to medical school was my objective, yet the starting point of this educational quest was quite distant. Initially, my task was to adopt an American mindset to assimilate into the system entirely. Later, I was informed about the slim likelihood of securing a place in medical school. With no medical professionals in my family tree, there was nobody to seek advice from.

My daily routes to various odd jobs would typically lead me past the prestigious universities I had only heard about growing up. *I can't help but wonder how these students manage to pay such exorbitant fees. They must come from wealthy families,* I often find myself musing.

Regarding supplication, my childhood was filled with spiritual gatherings steered by others. I'd shut my eyes and let the voices of my parents or other elders articulate cosmic pleas on my behalf. It was during these moments that I'd remind myself of my independence. Now, I played the role of both parent figures, which necessitated me learning to pray for myself and exercise faith, patience, and resilience. These were virtues instilled in me during my Christian high school education, initially for academic reasons, but now I had to apply these spiritual gifts in real-life scenarios.

Slowly but surely, I realized I wasn't fully grown but still somewhat mature. Occasionally, I contacted friends from high school who had made it to America before me. I would call these friends to learn how they cope with the new country. I hope that a great friend of brother status worth mentioning would often call and encourage me to move out of the bustling Washington DC suburb where I was to the quieter state of Alabama where focus on education could be easily achieved. This advice changed my life for good, as it set me on a path that led to the discovery of mentors, a vital component I lacked on my journey thus far.

During times of stress, I'd ignite the candle received at the send-off ceremony as a reminder that I was never truly isolated. As time passed, I discovered that incorporating meditation into my prayer routine could enhance my spiritual fortitude.

As I meditated, I often filled the silence with the harmonious sounds of classical music, primarily from instruments like the harp and piano. During several such instances, I'd find myself immersed in profound clarity that allowed me to witness the emergence of wisdom capable of untangling the problem at hand.

Throughout my development, I delved into the profundity of self-assertion and how it contributes to reaching our goals. I embody what I'm destined to become, which defines me more than the name I was given at birth.

The moment this realization dawned on me, I started addressing myself privately as a doctor, aligning my mentality with my purpose on a spiritual level, even before gaining admission into medical school. This proactive affirmation geared my mind and faith.

Lessons for Stability and Success

➤ **Adopt Change as an Opportunity for Growth**

Moving from a familiar environment to an entirely new one, from Africa to the United States, or any other transition, can be overwhelming. Rather than resisting the change, see it as a door to new opportunities. This shift is more than just geographical; it is a personal transformation that challenges your resilience, adaptability, and determination.

➤ **Know Your Financial Limits and Possibilities**

Financial awareness is key to stability in a new economic landscape. Take time to understand how to budget, save, and invest wisely. As you may have assisted in a family business back home, apply those lessons to manage your finances effectively. Being proactive in financial planning helps you avoid common pitfalls and makes it easier to build a stable future.

> ### Let Family Sacrifices Fuel Your Determination

If your loved ones have sacrificed to support your education or relocation, let that be a source of motivation rather than pressure. Honor their efforts by being diligent, committed, and purposeful in your pursuit of success. Their investment in you is financial and a belief in your potential.

> ### Transition from Dependency to Financial Independence

Taking on work to support your education or daily needs is more than a means of survival; it is a step toward self-reliance. No matter how small, every job contributes to your long-term financial stability. These responsibilities are stepping stones to independence and a chance to develop financial discipline.

➢ **Be Willing to Adjust and Relocate for Growth**

If your current environment does not support your academic or career aspirations, consider making necessary adjustments. Moving from a bustling city to a quieter place can sometimes create the focus needed for success. Be open to change and seek opportunities that align with your goals.Find Strength in Your Cultural and Spiritual Roots

Your background and traditions can serve as powerful anchors during difficult times. Whether through faith, family values, or cultural practices, these can offer comfort and guidance. Stay connected to what grounds you while remaining open to new experiences that help you grow.

➢ **Develop Self-Advocacy and Resilience**

The challenges you face, whether adjusting to a new education system, working multiple jobs, or applying to professional schools, can be daunting. However, these experiences shape you into a stronger, more self-sufficient individual. Learn to advocate for yourself, seek guidance, and persevere through obstacles.

Final Thought

The path to financial stability and personal success in a foreign land is never without challenges, but those challenges hold valuable lessons. Take control of your finances, honor your support system, and build resilience. You can confidently navigate financial hardship and cultural transitions.

Your story is still being written; make it one of perseverance and triumph.

CHAPTER THREE

THE HEALING PATH

In Africa, understanding the medical field is multifaceted and deeply entrenched in challenges impoverished communities face in accessing affordable and effective healthcare.

This chapter proves the transformative power of global health initiatives and the shared vision of making healthcare accessible and equitable for all. It's a chronicle of victories and setbacks, trials and triumphs, and the unwavering commitment to contributing to a healthier world.

Here, I will share my experiences, insights, and lessons learned, hoping to inspire and inform those who aspire to join this noble cause. It is a tale of resilience and resolve, compassion and commitment, and the quest to turn adversity into opportunity. Let's embark on this healing path together, uncovering the potential within each of us to make a significant difference in global health.

Medical School Experience

My medical and professional studies are one of transformation and growth. After years of rigorous medical training, I stepped into the 'real' world, faced with the harsh realities and complexities of the medical profession. Yet, I was not deterred. Instead, I was spurred on by a steadfast desire to alleviate suffering and bring healing to those in need.

My journey into medicine started with noble intentions, much like the countless others who expressed their spiritual calling and purpose during admission interviews. They professed a desire to help the sick and serve those in underserved communities. It was a privilege to witness such declarations of altruism and service.

However, over the years, I observed an alarming trend. Many medical students' initial enthusiasm and dedication seemed to wane as they became more aware of the sacrifices required to work in these resource-challenged communities. The mounting financial burden of their education often forced them to reconsider their decision to work in less lucrative, rural areas.

Yet, I wanted to repay the people and communities that raised me, and I stood firm and chose a different path. I refused to let materialistic considerations dictate my professional decisions. Despite being aware of the financial implications and hardships ahead, I remained steadfast in my commitment to serving those in need.

The world of healing was not just about treating physical ailments but about holistic healing encompassing health's physical, emotional, and spiritual dimensions. I advocated for building stronger relationships, improving communication, and sharing responsibilities between patients and clinicians.

My post-medical studies journey was a testament to my resilience and unwavering dedication to the noble cause of healing. I served in hard-to-reach communities, offering my medical expertise, empathetic understanding, and alternative healing practices. My journey is a compelling reminder of the true essence of medicine, a blend of art and technology dedicated to the service of humanity.

Choosing to Serve Rural and Poor Communities

In emerging economies, obtaining the same caliber of healthcare as in urban regions often imposes an insurmountable financial hurdle for rural dwellers.

In the Western world, third-party payers such as insurance firms and government entities mitigate this issue to a certain extent, which is typically absent in less developed nations.

Acknowledging that sustainable medical practice hinges on effective business strategies is crucial. Therefore, it's essential that in a medical facility, both business and healthcare delivery aspects distinctly and transparently present themselves to patients. This dual approach ensures smoother patient care and fosters a deeper patient-clinician relationship when monetary concerns aren't at the forefront of their interactions.

While this model, involving the patient, clinician, and third-party payer, is serving developed nations effectively, albeit with occasional adjustments, it urges healthcare providers in developing countries to innovate and design sustainable systems for the benefit of their patients.

Building on my story, I shall delve deeper into my motivations. Why did I choose to serve resource-strapped communities? The answer lies in my background. I hailed from such a community where the concept of immediate medical attention is often alien. Instead of rushing to hospitals, locals resort to homemade remedies and local concoctions, whose safety and efficacy are open to debate. This isn't a place with pharmaceutical chains at every corner, like what you'd find in the U.S.

Take the example of some villages. Here, traditional doctors practicing herbalism use plants and their extracts to treat ailments. While some swear by their effectiveness, concerns persist about long-term side effects, appropriate dosages, and potential drug interactions. These indigenous remedies require rigorous scientific research, which comes at a steep price and is often overlooked. Yet, amidst these challenges, unregulated local pharmaceutical entities thrive, offering affordable, albeit untested, solutions for various diseases. This reality in these communities is a stark reminder of the urgent need for sustainable and accessible evidence-based healthcare.

The potential to access foreign treatments renowned for their safety and effectiveness is within reach in an interconnected world. However, these solutions remain unattainable for many villagers living on the fringes of subsistence. Local pharmacies often dispense medicines based on a patient's financial capacity rather than a medically recommended dosage. This is a pervasive healthcare issue in communities grappling with poverty.

These villages lack emergency response infrastructure like ambulances, a crucial element in developed nations, leaving those needing care without immediate attention. Recognizing these healthcare challenges is the first critical step toward transforming these communities. The next is to devise a sustainable strategy that benefits all stakeholders and paves the way for equitable healthcare delivery, regardless of socioeconomic status. This approach can potentially revolutionize lives and introduce much-needed changes in these rural communities.

Being aware of these communities' trials and remaining passive, particularly for those originating from such areas, would be an act of disregard. It is our responsibility to uplift those in need, bring about, and be the change we wish to see. It is not merely about providing healthcare but empowering people to take charge of their health and well-being.

Every action taken, every choice made, is within cultural sensitivity and legal appropriateness. It's about respecting the community's traditions and beliefs while introducing them to modern medical practices that can enhance their quality of life.

This delicate balance is the cornerstone of sustainable change. In 2017, a significant milestone marked my journey. I became part of the prestigious Harvard Global Health Catalyst. This platform connected me with like-minded individuals and organizations passionate about reducing healthcare disparities. I had the opportunity to delve into the nuanced aspects of global health and understand the intricacies of bridging healthcare gaps.

The experience was about learning and collaborating to build lasting partnerships and platforms. It was about bringing together the intellectual prowess of academia, the innovative spirit of the business sector, the research-driven approach of pharmaceutical and clinical medicine, the structure of government policies, and the grassroots reach of non-governmental sectors.

I learned to leverage these diverse resources and expertise, all with the single goal of making healthcare accessible and equitable for all.

Many Africans have begun to understand the scope of the problem, from the reliance on traditional remedies to the glaring lack of emergency response infrastructure. My association with the Harvard Global Health Catalyst gave me a nuanced understanding of the potential solutions to bridge these healthcare gaps. My journey has underscored the critical role of collaboration across various sectors in driving sustainable change.

This journey involved me and the millions who struggle to access primary healthcare. It was a testament to the power of collaboration and the impact of a shared vision to revolutionize healthcare and transform lives in rural communities globally, one step at a time.

Financial Wisdom for a New Start

Adjusting to a new financial reality can be one of the most challenging transitions in life. Whether moving to a new country, navigating economic struggles, or striving for financial independence, the lessons you learn shape your future. Hardship is an opportunity to grow stronger, wiser, and more strategic in handling money and life.

These key takeaways are reflections and action points to help you build stability and success despite financial obstacles.

➤ Embrace Change as an Opportunity for Growth

Moving to a new place across countries or cities demands more than just physical relocation; it requires mental and financial adjustment. Instead of fearing change, embrace it as a chance to discover new opportunities. Success comes to those who adapt and find ways to thrive in unfamiliar environments. Approach every challenge with a learning mindset, knowing your resilience will shape your path.

> ➤ **Master Financial Awareness and Money Management**

Financial hardship often stems from not knowing how to manage money effectively in a new economic landscape. Take control of your finances by understanding your income, expenses, and savings potential. As you may have learned financial discipline through family responsibilities, apply the same principles now. Budget wisely, track your spending, and avoid debt traps that can derail your progress. A solid financial foundation starts with awareness and strategic planning.

> ➤ **Let Family Sacrifices Motivate You, Not Overwhelm You**

If your family has made sacrifices for your education, relocation, or financial well-being, use that as fuel for your ambition rather than a burden of expectation. Honor their efforts by working hard, staying focused, and maximizing your opportunities.

Their sacrifices are an investment in your success, so make it count.

> ➢ **Shift from Dependency to Financial Independence**

Becoming financially independent is not just about earning money; it's about managing it wisely. Whether you are taking on jobs to fund your education or sustain daily living, view them as stepping stones toward long-term self-sufficiency. Every effort you make today builds your ability to stand independently and create a stable future. Take pride in your ability to provide for yourself, no matter how small the start.

> ➢ **Be Willing to Relocate or Adjust for Better Opportunities**

Sometimes, your current location may not offer the best growth opportunities. If needed, be open to relocating where you can focus on education, career advancement, or financial stability. Moving from a fast-paced city to a quieter, more affordable area can provide the space needed to build your future.

Strategic moves, both financially and geographically, can make a significant difference to your success.

> ### Stay Rooted in Your Cultural and Spiritual Strengths

Your cultural background and personal beliefs are sources of strength. When facing challenges, draw wisdom from your traditions, faith, or values that have guided you in the past. These elements provide emotional and mental support, giving you the resilience to adapt while staying true to yourself. Even in unfamiliar territory, your roots can keep you grounded and focused.

> ### Build Resilience and Learn to Advocate for Yourself

Financial hardship teaches valuable lessons in perseverance and self-advocacy. Whether adjusting to a new education system, applying to schools, or seeking job opportunities, learning to speak up for yourself is essential. Be proactive in finding resources, asking for help, and pushing through obstacles. The ability to overcome setbacks separates those who succeed from those who stay stuck.

Final Thought

The Power to Shape Your Future Is in Your Hands.

Hardship is not the end of your story but the beginning of your transformation. The lessons you take from financial struggles will equip you with the mindset, discipline, and strategies needed for long-term success.

Question: Will you let financial hardship define you or use it to redefine your future?

The choice is yours. Take charge, make wise financial decisions, and turn challenges into stages for a secure and fulfilling life.

CHAPTER FOUR

LESSONS FROM THE FIELD

My initial vision was to attend to individual patients' health needs. However, as I explored the intricacies of healthcare provision, my perspective broadened, leading me to juxtapose U.S. healthcare with those found in developed and underdeveloped nations.

My fellowship with the esteemed Harvard Global Health Catalyst, a leading healthcare think tank dedicated to bridging the healthcare gap, further enriched my understanding of these disparities.

At this juncture in my career, I became acutely aware that my efforts, though noble, were insufficient to effect meaningful change, given the significant knowledge and resources at my disposal. This led me to venture into a more impactful role by joining the Kids of Tomorrow Foundation (KOT) and the KOT Foundation Hospital, serving as a healthcare consultant and director of health equity. Our mission was to cater to the health needs of orphans and refugees, particularly in the rural regions of Nigeria.

This experience gave me first-hand insights into the transformative potential of productive management of healthcare resources. To date, our team's contributions have led to the construction of a new hospital and the development of a health model that has garnered widespread admiration. The journey continues, however, as we strive to close the healthcare gap further and ensure equitable access to quality healthcare for all.

Bridging the Healthcare Gap Beyond Medicine

While serving as an internship physician in rural Nigeria, I've encountered many challenges rooted in cultural beliefs and practices.

Drawing from my experiences as a medical doctor working in rural African communities, I'd like to share a poignant incident from one of my missions in Nigeria. I encountered the heart-wrenching realities of healthcare in these areas at a modest hospital in a remote locale, partly funded through American grants.

Established initially as an HIV/AIDS treatment center, the hospital had expanded to include departments such as surgery, obstetrics-gynecology, and general medicine, thanks to the increased funding.

It was in 2022 when I, alongside my mentor, Dr. Chris, noticed the persistent stigma associated with HIV and its significant impact on the community. We had arrived carrying an assortment of medicines from the USA, intending to provide them free of charge to those in need. Eager to reach as many people as possible, we used the local radio station to broadcast our presence and mission.

However, the reality was far from what we had anticipated. We soon learned from local social workers and the patients themselves that our location, the HIV clinic, was a deterrent for many. They feared the societal assumption that visiting this hospital automatically labeled them as HIV-positive. It was a stark reminder of the additional barriers to healthcare that communities like this face, where the fear of stigma further increases the already wide healthcare gap.

This experience has further solidified my commitment to breaking down these barriers and ensuring that everyone, irrespective of their location or societal pressures, has access to the healthcare they deserve.

Another instance involved a typhoid outbreak in the region. A patient infected with enteric typhoid refused an antibiotic injection, a standard treatment protocol. He insisted on taking the medication in pill form, claiming needles couldn't penetrate his skin. I was unaware of this cultural belief, but later learned it was linked to a local voodoo practice known as *Odeshi*.

The nurse, more familiar with the local customs, took me aside and explained this belief to me. She imparted that *Odeshi* was a deeply ingrained practice in the community, causing deviations from typical medical norms. This cultural barrier, she explained, often hinders effective treatment and complicates our mission to provide adequate healthcare to this underserved population.

Despite this setback, we managed to treat the patient for malaria, another prevalent disease in the region. We also advised him on where to find us if he decided to accept the typhoid treatment.

This incident reminded us of the complex interplay of cultural beliefs and healthcare practices and the need for greater understanding and flexibility in our approach to medical aid in these communities.

These examples, like many I have experienced in my career, underscore the necessity of bridging the gap between modern medicine and traditional beliefs. They amplify the importance of cultural competence in healthcare delivery, especially in diverse rural communities. This is one of the many challenges we face in our mission to provide quality healthcare to all, regardless of their geographical or cultural circumstances.

Reducing the healthcare gap is not impossible but requires consistent effort. We must understand and strategize ways to overcome these persistent cultural barriers.

More recently, we went to a remote village in Nigeria after receiving an invitation from one of the political elites to assist his community. The news of our arrival had already spread as we arrived, and the locals eagerly awaited our presence. The village chief suggested we set up a temporary clinic in the community hall, which was the usual practice.

Adjacent to the community hall, where we parked our medical outreach van, there stood a shrine. We were intrigued by its presence but knew better than to approach it, as we understood the importance of respecting the local culture and traditions. Our primary purpose in the village was to offer medical treatment, not to interfere with their rituals.

We did not realize our presence had already impacted the shrine, and word had spread about this unexpected occurrence. Consequently, a group of shrine members visited our clinic out of curiosity, wanting to observe if our medicines were as effective as their traditional remedies.

On that day, they were preparing a potion to combat yellow fever, intending to share it with the village. However, the shrine members believed that our presence may have diminished the spiritual potency of their herbal medicine. Despite this, our team diligently treated numerous patients and scheduled additional appointments for the following day.

The following day, we were astonished to find a lush tree with vibrant green leaves in front of the shrine next to where we had parked our medical outreach van the day before, wholly desiccated and devoid of a single leaf. Additionally, my team observed that the earthen pot placed on one of its branches the day before had been replaced by a different pot.

These peculiar details sparked conversations amongst our team as we continued to care for the patients that day. What had transpired was an inexplicable transformation, evidently due to our presence. It had a profound impact on the local culture and spiritual practices. We observed first-hand interaction between Western and traditional medical approaches within the context of the respective cultures that influence them.

Like many before, it reminds us of the interconnectedness between healthcare and the broader cultural context, urging us to approach our work with sensitivity and respect for our communities' beliefs and traditions.

Later, in the afternoon of our second day in the village, an older man, a member of the local shrine, came to us with a leg wound that indicated potential uncontrolled diabetes. We had a sufficient supply of Metformin, a medication used to treat diabetes, brought from the USA. We had enough to treat all the diabetics in this village and beyond.

One of my team members, a local social worker, gave me an acknowledging wink. I initially interpreted this as a gesture of mutual respect, a wordless *'well done'* exchange between us. However, the ensuing interaction with the patient would soon reveal the true meaning of his gesture.

As we assessed his condition, the elderly patient, addressing me as *'Docci,'* a term of endearment for a doctor, made a surprising request. He implored me not to pay attention to his wound, insisting that he had come for treatment of Malaria. I was taken aback; how could I possibly ignore a wound in such a condition that required medical attention?

Sensing my confusion, the social worker took me aside to explain the cultural significance of the wound. It was not an ordinary wound, he told me; it was what the locals were referring to as a *'night gun'* wound.

This was a form of supernatural infliction, a punitive measure observed by shrine members. At this point, I wondered what our punishment could be since we had 'inadvertently disturbed them' by practicing

PRESCRIPTIONS FOR SUCCESS

Western-influenced medicine in the vicinity of their shrine. Despite my shock, I mustered the courage to continue attending to the patient, considering the cultural sensitivities that had just been unveiled. As I later learned, the shrine members were allowed to seek Western medicines to treat illnesses for which they had no remedies.

I am on a quest to bridge the gap in healthcare, yet I find myself discovering anomalies within this gap that were never part of my medical school curriculum.

The elderly man stated, "Doc, it's not diabetes; my A1C level has consistently been under 5.5. Feel free to verify it if you wish."

And indeed, we did repeatedly; his claim stood accurate. A1C level is the quickest method to diagnose diabetes, with a score of 6.5 or higher indicating a positive result.

Surprisingly, for a layman, his knowledge exceeded the norm. Then, I realized that mere medication and medical procedures were insufficient to bridge this gap. Culture was an integral part of this gap and was impossible to overlook.

The Healing Component of Diagnosis and Treatment.

A severe health problem can disrupt all aspects of your life, whether it's a chronic or life-threatening illness, such as cancer, or a major health emergency, such as a stroke, heart attack, or debilitating injury. Many serious health problems seem to develop unexpectedly, upsetting your life out of the blue. You may feel overwhelmed by waves of complex emotions from fear and worry to profound sadness, despair, and grief, or just numbness, frozen by shock or the feeling that you'll never be able to cope.

The emotional upheaval can make it difficult to function or think straight and even lead to mood disorders such as anxiety and depression. Not only do patients experience daily difficulties in dealing with the symptoms of a disease, but there is the added weight of bearing the new label that has been given to them as an owner of the disorder to carry and to do so for life, as the case with chronic illnesses would prove.

But whatever your diagnosis or emotional response, it's essential to know you're not powerless. There are steps you can take to better cope with your new situation, ease the stress and mental anguish that often accompany serious illness, and find a way to navigate this challenging new expedition.

The human body is a complex system that often requires medical intervention to restore balance. The healing journey is progressive, starting with a diagnosis, moving through treatment, and ending with recovery. This path is an integral part of medicine and is crucial in promoting patient health and fostering healing.

Diagnosis: The Crucial First Step

The first step towards healing is diagnosis. This is where the healthcare professionals identify the cause of the patient's symptoms. Initially, in this step, the clinician must listen attentively as the patient describes the symptoms, a process called acquiring patient history. A collection of symptoms usually creates suspicion for a couple of likely diagnoses, known as the differential diagnoses.

Narrowing the list to an accurate diagnosis can involve numerous tests and examinations. This process may involve a multidisciplinary approach in some situations, requiring specialized input from several medical experts. When done correctly, it is the same process used to find the root cause of any problem. Without a proper diagnosis, any subsequent treatments may not be effective, as they do not target the actual cause.

Treatment: The Active Phase of Healing

Once a diagnosis has been made, the next step is treatment, usually presented or documented as a plan of action. Depending on the nature of the ailment, this could involve medication, surgery, physiotherapy, or other interventions. The goal of treatment is to address the root cause identified in the diagnosis, alleviate the patient's symptoms, and maintain them on a continuously improving status as much as possible while they recover.

In this phase, medical professionals actively intervene to restore the patient's health. A well-planned and executed treatment is vital in putting the patient on the path of recovery. After the medical team has done its part, success in this phase depends on the patient's compliance with the proposed treatment plan.

Recovery: The Final Milestone

Finally, it's the recovery phase, where healing manifests. This is when the body starts regaining its normal function after an illness or injury. It's not just about physical healing. Recovery also encompasses the mental and emotional aspects of healing.

During this phase, patients often need ongoing support to manage lingering symptoms or side effects from the treatment. Only when patients progress through this phase do they genuinely heal. In this phase, many attest to a spiritual component in healing. The experience reported in this phase differs from one patient to the next.

Healing is a process that requires time, patience, and appropriate medical intervention. It starts with a correct diagnosis, leading to effective treatment, and finally culminates in recovery. Without this structured approach, proper healing may remain elusive. Healthcare providers must guide their patients through these stages, ensuring they understand the process and are actively involved in their healing journey. This comprehensive approach ensures that the path to healing is not just about disease management but also about promoting overall well-being.

Medical Challenges (Technology and social media)

Limited Access to Advanced Medical Technology

One of the significant challenges facing African doctors is the scarcity of advanced medical technology. This inadequacy means that many medical facilities are under-equipped, thus limiting diagnostic capabilities and treatment options. High-tech equipment like MRI machines, CT scanners, and advanced laboratory equipment are scarce.

This situation hinders accurate diagnosis and appropriate treatment, leading to poor health outcomes. In areas with this equipment, there is still the challenge of very high-cost maintenance, hence the difficulty in sustainability.

Lack of Adequate Training and Knowledge

Due to the limited availability of advanced medical technology, many healthcare professionals lack the training to operate these machines effectively. This lack of knowledge can lead to misdiagnosis and improper treatment, further exacerbating the healthcare crisis.

Unequal Distribution of Healthcare Resources

Even in places with access to technology, it is often unequally distributed, with urban areas having significantly more resources than rural areas. This disparity leads to inequitable healthcare delivery, leaving those in rural areas behind.

Lack of Reliable Internet Access

While social media and digital platforms have the potential to improve health outcomes through telemedicine and health education, the lack of reliable and affordable internet access in many parts of Africa hinders this progress. This digital divide limits doctors' ability to consult with colleagues, access up-to-date medical information, and provide telemedicine services.

Misinformation on Social Media

While social media can be a powerful tool for disseminating health information, it can also be a source of misinformation. Misleading information about diseases, treatments, and prevention can spread quickly, leading to confusion and potentially harmful health behaviors.

Most users of these platforms have little or no experience differentiating between reputable sources of information and those that are not. They often mistake mere opinions for formal medical peer-reviewed, research-backed, and evidence-based information.

As mentioned earlier, the challenges profoundly impact poorer African communities. Limited access to advanced medical technology and a lack of adequately trained healthcare professionals significantly hampers healthcare quality. The inability to diagnose and treat conditions effectively can lead to higher morbidity and mortality rates and lower life expectancy.

The unequal distribution of healthcare resources often leaves rural and poorer communities underserved, leading to health inequities. Individuals in these communities may have to travel long distances to access healthcare, which can be costly and time-consuming.

The digital divide and misinformation on social media can also lead to a lack of accurate health information and limited access to telemedicine services. This situation can exacerbate health disparities and contribute to poor health outcomes in these communities.

We must strive to invest in advanced medical technology and training, improve internet access, and leverage social media for accurate health information dissemination.

Broaden Your Professional and Social Impact

> Expand Your Perspective as You Grow

When entering any profession, your focus may initially be on mastering individual skills and tasks. However, as you gain experience, be open to seeing how your work contributes to the well-being of communities and societies. A broader perspective allows you to step beyond personal ambition and into roles that create lasting impact.

> Turn Challenges into Catalysts for Innovation

Disparities and inefficiencies exist in every field, but instead of being discouraged, they see them as opportunities for innovation. Your response to these challenges can drive meaningful changes in healthcare, education, or any sector. The most significant transformations often start with small, purposeful actions that align with a greater mission, like the work done with the Kids of Tomorrow Foundation.

> ## Master Cultural Competence and Local Engagement

Working in diverse environments, particularly rural or culturally distinct areas, requires more than technical expertise. Understanding and respecting local customs, traditions, and belief systems can determine how your services are received. Approach each community humbly, listen actively, and adapt your strategies to build trust and effectiveness. Communication is just as important as the service you provide.

> ## Bridge the Gap Between Tradition and Modernity

Many communities have strong cultural and traditional beliefs that shape their healthcare, business, and education perspectives. Rather than dismissing these beliefs as obstacles, learn how to integrate local wisdom with modern advancements. This approach can help ease the adoption of new practices while respecting the values of the communities you serve.

➤ Collaborate and Build Meaningful Partnerships

You cannot create lasting change alone. Partnering with local leaders, institutions, and global organizations strengthens your reach and enhances your effectiveness. Initiatives like those with the Harvard Global Health Catalyst show the power of collaboration in tackling widespread issues. Whether working on small projects or large-scale initiatives, teamwork amplifies impact.

➤ Embrace a Lifelong Learning Mindset

Every career experience offers valuable lessons, both expected and unexpected. Challenges teach adaptability, failures build resilience, and successes reinforce effective strategies. Whether providing direct services, managing resources, or educating others, each moment adds to your professional and personal growth. Approach your work with curiosity and a willingness to evolve.

Final Thought

Your profession is a career and tool for change. You can move beyond personal success to create a broader, lasting impact by expanding your vision, embracing challenges, respecting cultural contexts, and fostering collaboration.

Your work matters. Your actions count. Your ability to adapt and innovate can change lives. Keep learning, keep growing, and keep making a difference.

CHAPTER FIVE

THE KIDS OF TOMORROW FOUNDATION

The Kids of Tomorrow Foundation is a non-profit organization established in 2019. Its primary mission is to provide care to orphaned children in Eastern Nigeria. The foundation aims to improve the lives of these children by focusing on their basic needs and ensuring they receive primary education. Since its inception, the foundation has made a significant impact, reaching out to over 30,000 children through its various programs. These programs are implemented in over 200 rural and urban Eastern Nigeria locations.

For me, studying medicine and acquiring business knowledge has had a significant positive impact on how I have been able to assist rural and poor communities. My medical knowledge enables me to provide essential healthcare services, tackle prevalent diseases, and promote health awareness. A deep understanding of the importance of medicine has meant I have been able to facilitate personalized care, which is crucial in rural areas where access to specialized care may be limited.

On the other hand, my business knowledge has aided in efficiently managing healthcare resources. It has helped devise strategies to overcome financial limitations, improve the quality of care, and address private concerns. Business acumen has also helped and contributed to building my partnerships, securing funding, and implementing sustainable healthcare models in these communities.

I genuinely believe that knowing these areas has acted as a bridge between myself as a healthcare provider and the community. It has led to initiatives to enhance health literacy, which is often a barrier to healthcare access in impoverished areas. By addressing the unique healthcare challenges of these communities, these dual skills have significantly improved population health and patient well-being.

The Best of Both Worlds

As a dedicated medical professional and a profound admirer of business strategy, I have found myself in a unique position where I can intertwine these two domains to make a significant difference in the world. My involvement with the Kids of Tomorrow Foundation Hospital and Wellness Center provides me with the perfect platform to deploy my blend of skills and experience.

The KOT Foundation Hospital and Wellness Center is a remarkable initiative born by the Kids of

Tomorrow Foundation. This humanitarian organization illuminates the future of underprivileged communities with hope, possibilities, and progress.

The organization's inception was marked by a focus on offering shelter to orphaned children. However, as the foundation grew, so did its ambit and objectives. Today, it stands as a beacon of hope and nurture, providing shelter, a supportive home, a promising future, and quality education to displaced and orphaned children living in the eastern region of Nigeria.

In this inspiring organization, I have been entrusted with the roles of Healthcare Consultant and Director of Health Equity. These roles allow me to marry my medical expertise and business acumen to best serve the community. I am tasked with guiding the foundation toward achieving its lofty goals and laying the groundwork for expanding access to affordable healthcare beyond the confines of our immediate community.

I aim to utilize my unique blend of skills to help the board of directors implement a scalable and sustainable healthcare model. By doing so, we strive to close the healthcare gap and provide quality, affordable healthcare services to a broader population.

The journey is challenging yet rewarding. As we continue strategizing and implementing, we are constantly learning and evolving. It is a unique opportunity to contribute to a mission's medical and business aspects, fundamentally serving humanity and creating a brighter future for those most in need.

My role at the KOT Foundation Hospital and Wellness Center is a testament to how the confluence of medical knowledge and business understanding can fuel transformative change. It's a journey of discovery, service, and growth, and I am privileged to be a part of it.

As a physician at the KOT Foundation Hospital, my contributions span various aspects of the organization's operations. I primarily aid the leadership by interpreting and utilizing epidemiological data from renowned health organizations like the Centers for Disease Control and the World Health Organization. This data influences our strategy for preventing and treating both communicable and non-communicable diseases, providing an informed base to determine which medications are most necessary for our unique patient demographic.

Beyond this, I also play a crucial role in sourcing essential medications for our hospital. Through concerted efforts, I have secured donations from charitable organizations such as Kingsway Charities and the Catholic Medical Mission Board (CMMB). These donations significantly augment our medical relief missions, particularly in the underserved communities of Nigeria.

As part of an international team of health professionals, I have participated in medical missions to the Cross River and Taraba States in Nigeria. Our focus during these missions is to provide immediate medical aid and educate the communities about crucial health aspects like proper nutrition, personal hygiene, disease prevention, and treatment. This holistic approach to healthcare helps instill a culture of health consciousness within these communities.

My contributions to the KOT Foundation Hospital also extend into fostering strategic partnerships. For instance, I spearheaded the creation of a collaboration between our hospital and the Gechaan Medical Center for HIV/AIDS located in Taraba State, Nigeria. This partnership not only provides medication support to the medical center but also allows for the expansion of their patient care services to include non-communicable diseases. This broadening impact reflects my commitment to improving healthcare access and quality in Nigeria, regardless of the challenges.

Sustainable Solutions from the Kids of Tomorrow Foundation

> ### Integrate Diverse Skills for Greater Impact

Bringing together expertise from different fields enhances effectiveness when uplifting underprivileged communities. Combining medical knowledge, business acumen, and strategic management can significantly improve healthcare delivery and resource distribution. True progress is achieved when diverse skills work together to create holistic, sustainable solutions.

> ### Empower Communities Through Education

Knowledge is a powerful tool for breaking cycles of poverty and disease. By prioritizing primary education and health literacy, you help individuals make informed decisions about their well-being. In regions with limited access to healthcare, education becomes a preventive measure empowering people to recognize symptoms, seek timely treatment, and adopt healthier lifestyles.

> **Bridge Gaps Between Different Sectors**

The most effective interventions do not operate in isolation. Leveraging interdisciplinary approaches, whether connecting healthcare with business strategies, social work with medical outreach, or technology with fieldwork, leads to comprehensive and sustainable community solutions. Identifying and filling gaps between sectors creates stronger and more efficient support systems for those in need.

> **Build Strong Partnerships to Expand Your Reach**

Strategic collaborations amplify meaningful change. Partnerships with organizations like Kingsway Charities and the Catholic Medical Mission Board (CMMB) have provided crucial medical resources, enabling wider healthcare accessibility.

Expanding networks with like-minded organizations, donors, and policymakers strengthens long-term impact.

> ## Use Data-Driven Approaches for Maximum Effectiveness

Relying on trusted epidemiological data from CDC, WHO, and other global health organizations ensures that initiatives are well-informed and effective. Understanding disease prevalence, community-specific health challenges, and successful intervention models allows for targeted and evidence-based action plans that drive real results.

> ## Address Both Communicable and Non-Communicable Diseases

Effective healthcare strategies must address the full spectrum of health challenges. Many underserved communities face a dual burden of infectious diseases such as malaria, tuberculosis, and HIV, alongside rising cases of diabetes, hypertension, and cardiovascular diseases. A well-rounded approach considering immediate and long-term health needs ensures comprehensive and equitable healthcare.

> ## ➤ Advocate for Scalable and Sustainable Healthcare Models

The true impact extends beyond a single mission or project. Pushing for scalable, adaptable healthcare models ensures that interventions are temporary fixes and long-term solutions that can benefit multiple communities over time. Whether through policy advocacy, healthcare system reforms, or replicable community programs, creating lasting change requires forward-thinking strategies.

Final Thought

The Kids of Tomorrow Foundation exemplifies what is possible when innovation, education, healthcare, and collaboration intersect. By integrating diverse skills, fostering partnerships, leveraging data, and promoting education, you can contribute to sustainable solutions that transform entire communities.

Your work today can shape a healthier, more resilient future. Stay committed, stay informed, and strive for meaningful, long-lasting change.

CHAPTER SIX

THE POWER OF CHOICE

Everything I have accomplished in life has come down to my choices. It would be unfair to say that I have been able to make positive impacts on communities because life was 'easy.' It most certainly wasn't, and countless times, I have found myself in challenging situations about making the right choice to hopefully provide me with an intended outcome.

It's essential to remember that you, like me, are the architect of your life and that the power of choice lies solely in your hands. It might be convenient to shift the responsibility onto others, but the truth remains that your own decisions drive your feelings, actions, and results.

Perhaps during childhood, you preferred reading rather than cleaning up after yourself. When you made that choice, you disengaged from what others perceived as laziness.

Perhaps, later in life, you again choose to suppress your desires to maintain harmony with your partner, sideline your book project for household chores, or soften your assertiveness at work following criticism from your boss.

Each of these decisions reflects your autonomy. They significantly influence who you transform into and the kind of life you lead. The freedom to choose feelings, actions, desires, behavior, beliefs, or your presence in the world is a divine gift. A careful introspection of your life will reveal a trail of choices you have consciously or subconsciously made until this very moment.

If the reflection in the mirror doesn't, please remember you always have the power to choose differently next time. Every situation presents an array of options.

Whether to stay in a toxic relationship or leave, chase your ambition of becoming a doctor or stick with your current occupation, rise from bed at the sound of the alarm or keep hitting snooze, or choose between eating a salad or a bowl of ice cream - these are all choices and the outcomes of which we must deal with, whether with satisfaction or not.

You are constantly presented with choices. This implies that you can always choose, and every decision further empowers you. Decide on the person you wish to evolve into and what you aspire to possess. Once you have clarity on these, your choices regarding the course of action to adopt become natural and informed, encompassing what changes need to be implemented.

The Paradox of Choice

Imagine that you urgently need milk, so you dash to the supermarket. Upon reaching the chilled dairy section, you're confronted with various selections. It's not just about deciding the fat percentage anymore. You're also faced with determining the source of the milk: cow, almond, soy, or oat, among other varieties. You are rooted to the spot in this sea of choices, clueless about which milk to opt for. The sheer multitude of options has left you feeling overwhelmed. You may even begin to doubt the knowledge you've acquired thus far concerning milk.

This scenario illustrates what is termed as 'the *paradox of choice,*' a growing issue in our modern society where accessibility to an increasing number of alternatives is on the rise. The paradox of choice proposes an intriguing notion. While we may assume that being offered a wide array of options simplifies finding one that we are content with, thereby boosting consumer satisfaction, the reality can be quite different. An overabundance of choices necessitates tremendous decision-making effort and can result in dissatisfaction with our final selection.

Let's say the supermarket stocks full-cream milk and low-fat milk. For many, that decision is much easier to make. You may straightforwardly assess the benefits and drawbacks of both options that suit you and your preferences. However, discerning the best choice becomes much more complex when the possibilities multiply.

An exciting paradox suggests that excess choices inhibit rather than enhance our liberation. The cornerstone of Western civilizations, particularly the United States, is liberty. This liberty is frequently linked to the concept of options, with the presumption that more options equate to greater freedom.

The rationale is straightforward: rather than being compelled to select from a couple of alternatives, individuals can choose from a virtually infinite array of possibilities. Businesses and corporations often embrace this ideology, believing that a broader range of choices will enhance customer satisfaction.

Nonetheless, in today's world, this unprecedented abundance of choices has ironically led to individuals being less content with their decisions. Instead of bolstering decision satisfaction, an excess of options tends to diminish the likelihood of individuals feeling content with their final decision. While liberty is paramount, a delicate balance exists between having the freedom to choose as you please and feeling overwhelmed by an excess of options.

The dilemma of choosing from an abundance of alternatives is not solely a worrying element for economics and consumer gratification but also a problem increasingly appearing in diverse aspects of our lives as our choices approach an infinite scope.

In addition, the advent of the internet and social media platforms has simplified the process of exploring various options available to us, eliminating the need to visit a store to evaluate our alternatives physically. The rapid progression in technology and scientific fields further implies a constant emergence of new job types, let alone the myriads of job opportunities (such as influencers, social media experts, etc.) created by several social media applications.

And where the paradox of choice comes into play is for people who are *optimizers.* If you are the person who continuously focuses on making sure you always make the 'best' choice rather than just settling for an option you find satisfactory, making choices can be difficult.

When presented with myriad options, it likely becomes increasingly difficult for you to discern the best one, often leading to considerable stress and remorse after a decision. Furthermore, when the number of choices increases, so does the potential for missed opportunities, which can intensify feelings of regret. The irony of choice is that the many options available induce stress and ultimately lead to a sensation of confined discontentment.

A further irony lies in how choice allocates responsibility to the decision-maker. When presented with a single option, you accept what's available. However, when faced with numerous alternatives, one ends up being unhappy with their selection...well, the only person left to point fingers at is yourself.

At this point, I can't help but reflect on life while growing up in Africa, where our prayers focused on solving the lack of options. It is a far cry from my world today, where I pray not to be caught up in the wrong choice, as the possibilities are just too many.

As a civilization, we have an excess of options compared to our forebears. Our celebration of freedom to choose has profound implications for our cultural roots. Take relationships, for example; we are choosing to gradually lose the societal expectation for marriage through our actions. Similarly, more individuals aren't motivated or patient enough to stick to a single profession until retirement, as was the case some decades ago. These myriad choices often leave us questioning whether we've made the right decision.

The old approach to choice wasn't all bad after all. The strategy of using predetermined paths, as was done back in the day, could have been restrictive, but they provided a certain sense of security. Decision-making was externally controlled, at least to an extent. And whenever we found ourselves pigeonholed into roles we didn't enjoy, the blame was placed on societal structures, not us.

In addition, in today's world, if one prioritizes a career over family and later regrets their decision while watching their contemporaries nurture their offspring, the remorse is potent, and self-blame is the usual response. After all, it was a decision made by the individual.

Working Through Choice Overload

With the progression of society, science, and technology, we are presented with a broader array of choices. This plethora of options can easily lead to confusion, resulting in choice overload. When we encounter excessive possibilities, the decision-making process is hampered. The abundance of choices impairs our ability to make a sound decision and affects our contentment with the conclusion we eventually arrive at.

Contrary to our forebears, we don't conclude our day contented that we executed our tasks well; instead, we finalize it by scanning through our emails *one last time, just for good measure,* and with a sigh, we acknowledge to ourselves that there was more to be done. People say 24 hours isn't enough for a day; they need more time!

If you're conscious of the influence choices exert on you, you can strive to counteract it. Diminish stress over trivial decisions and stand firm on more significant ones. This is a comparatively recent dilemma for our species, and the repercussions are unfolding. Remember how your decisions affect your emotional state and make choices judiciously.

Every so often, we need to do a mental clean-up, examining all the ideas, projects, and activities we've gotten ourselves into. We should reduce the list and ensure that only what is important is focused on. This personal check and balance is essential for a healthy mind. This exercise will train the mind to reduce our focus on unnecessary endeavors if done right and often.

A crowded mind is comparable to hoarding. To hoarders, most things they encounter are essential and may be helpful someday, so they hold on to them. The plethora of options and the divine right to choose from them is responsible for mental hoarding; globalization has introduced this condition into otherwise free cultures. Not all ideas that come to mind are worth pursuing, as entertaining or lucrative as they may seem.

Which ideas are worth our time and consideration? You may ask. It all boils down to goal setting. Ideas that contribute to achieving one's goal are those to keep and prioritize. Therefore, those with no set goals will find themselves entertaining and accepting ideas left and right, and there goes the hoarding.

There is a difficulty with choosing that most commonly occurs when we have to make decisions about subjects, we lack sufficient understanding of. This effect tends to lessen as our familiarity with the topic increases. For instance, a professional baker wouldn't struggle to select a variety of flour. Similarly, even if you're not an expert on snack chips, your basic understanding ensures you're not overwhelmed by the broad selection at the grocery store.

The concept of willpower is akin to our physical stamina, although it's applied to decision-making rather than physical exertion. Just as physical activities like exercise or work can tire out your muscles, each decision you make, no matter how minor, puts a strain on your brain and depletes your reserve of willpower for future decisions. This is why we tend to lose willpower or drive when we are mentally exhausted.

Physical exercise serves as an excellent analogy here. When you initiate your fitness routine, your muscles are in their optimal state, capable of reaching a set performance level. If you exert yourself excessively, your energy levels deplete, and your muscles begin to tire.

As your glucose and mineral reserves dwindle, your capacity and desire continue to wane until you eventually halt and allow yourself some respite. Or you may overexert yourself, leading to reckless injury. This concept perfectly parallels the functioning of willpower in your brain and mind.

Initially, your decision-making capacity is at its zenith, and adhering to your choices comes naturally. However, each decision you make and maintain exhausts your mental strength and diminishes the impact of each subsequent choice you need to make.

To manage and avoid being overwhelmed, your brain begins to simplify its processes, discarding what it deems as non-crucial elements to lessen the complexity; you may even start taking things for granted at this point because you're not the most efficient. You're in survival mode. Therefore, if physical rest replenishes the muscle's ability to reengage in physical activity, mental rest will do the same for the brain and mind.

The burden of decision-making is inherently linked to the time you must make those choices. Under time constraints, the burden of choice intensifies: the decision becomes more challenging and nerve-wracking, and ultimately, you are less content with the outcome, especially in unfamiliar circumstances.

Studies suggest that when you make decisions under time pressure, you will likely be less content with the outcomes and may often experience a sense of regret. This feeling emerges when your mind believes it could have made a better selection if given more time and starts to amplify all the negatives.

The most effective strategy in such circumstances is to step away and allow yourself additional time. Allocate more time to contemplate and assess all available alternatives before concluding but avoid lingering excessively.

Being early in your endeavors allows for the advantage of setting a relaxed deadline and avoiding time constraints. By setting a relaxed deadline for reaching a decision, you can reduce remorse and alleviate the discomfort associated with decision-making. However, some situations call for a hard decision deadline, and there isn't time to think for some.

Medical emergencies, for example, call for swift choice and decision-making, and a debrief (collective thinking and feedback) is done afterward. This is why rehearsals are essential to train the mind to make the right decisions swiftly and repeatedly under unfavorable conditions such as time constraints. This decision-making ability is a cornerstone of the medical training curriculum.

Segmenting is a potent tool to combat choice overload. Indeed, you have encountered this tactic, as it is universally applied, from academia to research and corporations like Airbnb. The core of this strategy lies in dividing decisions into several separate stages, making them more approachable and manageable.

Suppose you are organizing a holiday to Africa and require accommodation. You navigate the Airbnb website, search for an appropriate option, and key in *Nigeria*; suddenly, you're swamped with hundreds of propositions. This is a classic scenario of choice overload.

However, Airbnb doesn't abandon you in this sea of options they understand the effect of being overwhelmed. Consequently, they promptly provide you with a range of topical filters to dissect the proposals into comprehensible "segments," each one progressively refining and narrowing down your choices.

Are you seeking a location at a central spot? Would you prefer a full kitchen, or need somewhere to sleep? The often-challenging task of selecting the ideal lodging is simplified to a few binary choices by pressing several buttons. This process filters down the options to a small selection that can be quickly reviewed. Therefore, with segmentation, the desired action, which in this case is renting a house, arrives much quicker and with less stress than otherwise.

Each offer displays a large image up front, providing an immediate sense of the accommodation's atmosphere. This ignites a sensory experience of finding the right place instead of deciding solely based on logical reasoning.

You can take the same approach to all the choices you need to make, whether you are just trying to buy some milk or making long-term decisions about your career or investments.

Choices Have Outcomes

The outcomes you experience are directly influenced by the decisions you make. The responsibility rests solely on your shoulders. The decision to peruse this piece is yours, just as you will decide to accept or reject the guidance from my "external" voice. I've navigated this journey before and have faced numerous failures due to poor decisions and adopting an "I can't" mindset rather than "I can."

The path to success is paved with trials and errors, and I have many. Some days excel over others. We can only control a handful of elements in our lives. Still, these few aspects of our thoughts, emotions, choices, and actions are sufficient to significantly differentiate whichever path we embark on. Time is not an ally in this journey.

Your life is yours to steer, and your choice is ultimately yours. Remember that the outcome of good decisions will always be good when allowed to take its course. Life, in general, is a long-term game. Don't be too quick to conclude that the outcome of an endeavor is a failure. Be patient if your decisions and actions concerning the matter are good.

Thoughts

There are primarily two types of thoughts we encounter: the ones that echo within our mind, which I term internal voices, and those that stem from others, known as external voices.

Let's first tackle these external voices; they can be exceedingly harmful, as they can lead you to believe that your only option is to heed their words. The most impactful external voices usually arise from two sectors: individuals you confide in and those who wield authority (either due to their experience, status, or both).

This includes (un)solicited feedback given to you with the expectation that you will use them to ensure your growth. In these instances, the decision rests on whether you heed these voices. Those I trust or care for often desire my best interests, shielding me from disappointment, humiliation, or harm. In numerous situations, these individuals have never endeavored to do what I was attempting to do. Hence, it's your prerogative to accept their advice or not.

This principle also applies to the voices of authority, such as supervisors, educators, medical professionals, and so on. Opting not to heed the advice of these authoritative figures can lead to repercussions (it's not always advisable to disregard expert advice unless you possess knowledge unknown to them).

The ultimate decision, however, of accepting their viewpoints and their sway rests with you.

These external influences have the power to shape your internal dialogues. The thought within can either be constructive or destructive. You can decide whether the perception of others or your beliefs determines your limitations. It's entirely up to you if you allow circumstances beyond your control to dictate your capabilities and restrictions or even the way you feel.

Feelings

Your beliefs, actions, and emotional tone are within your grasp. The direction of your attention determines your emotions. If there's a downpour outside, you can label it as a dreadful day, or a day filled with potential. Note that everyone around you doesn't perceive the situation like you do. Note that rain is not welcomed by those planning a picnic but is a blessing to the farmer.

How you feel is up to you. Of course, there's a footnote to this statement; there are individuals who battle severe depression, yet medical professionals can often aid in these cases. It is imperative to note that how we feel is linked to how we interpret our experiences. For example, on a field day, we volunteered at a soup kitchen that fed a large population of unhoused individuals.

A good friend I was with lost his wallet and some cash at this event. When we were chatting about it, his approach to the loss was somewhat different; he said that the money in his lost wallet would provide one of these people with more than just soup, and he was glad it would. And to him, it wasn't worth looking for this lost money; he let it go. I should tell you at this point that he has a calm and collected mindset and approaches stress; unlike most people I know.

However, our sentiments are ours to pick from, given that we base those decisions on where we wish to direct our attention. If you desire a setback to lead to feelings of despair, then dwell on all the mistakes you made and the resources you squandered. Conversely, if you wish for a setback to inspire optimism, follow in the footsteps of Thomas Edison and numerous other inventors by telling yourself, "I've just found out one way my idea won't succeed; that's progress."

One emotional gateway shuts while another unveils your decision and your prerogative. Take informed actions and embrace the outcome with a mindset to learn and teach from the experience; that is leadership!

Actions

Your emotions and thoughts vie for control, dictating your actions. The term 'work' can be defined as the product of mass, acceleration, and distance. Essentially, it represents your capacity to act. The real difficulty lies in not allowing your physical state or pessimistic thoughts to hinder your determination to persevere. Are you exhausted?

The decision to either continue or step back is entirely yours. I advise that when it comes to our work or any form of action, we must identify what motivates us to do it in the first place. This factor ensures diligent effort when a setback or discouragement occurs.

For your physical health and capacity for continuous effort, you need to make a conscious decision to fortify your bodily strength. It's important to acknowledge that you have physiological limitations, and improving your endurance requires time. The most crucial decision to make here is to commit to physical fitness, work towards achieving it, and maintain it consistently.

When you engage in this activity, an interesting phenomenon occurs - your body generates hormones that enhance your cognitive functions and elevate your mood, potentially creating a positive chain reaction that propels you closer to achieving your objectives. There is a great chain of events that cycles on itself.

When we make good choices, we feel good. Feeling good creates a healthy mindset, which motivates us to make even more suitable choices. Physical exercise, for example, makes us feel good and promotes good overall health. Good health and a good mood are vital for further exercise and making great choices.

It's up to you to decide whether to keep your body active. The food you consume, and the duration of your rest are also under your control. The three primary elements influencing your body's efficiency are rest, diet, and physical activity. It's not a complex concept the challenge lies in maintaining consistency amidst many other choices, thoughts, and emotions that can be distracting!

You are at your best when your choices are correct. The choice you make in anything concerning you affects everything concerning you.

Take Control of Your Life

> ➤ **Your Choices Shape Your Life's Trajectory**

Every decision big or small plays a role in determining your future. You are the architect of your life, and the choices you make today will influence the opportunities, relationships, and experiences you encounter tomorrow. Whether it's choosing a career, nurturing relationships, or forming daily habits, every choice builds the foundation of your success. Taking ownership of your decisions empowers you to stop blaming external factors and take proactive steps toward your goals.

> ### More Choices Don't Always Lead to Better Outcomes

The paradox of choice reveals that an excess of options can lead to decision fatigue and dissatisfaction. While options are valuable, too many can make decision-making overwhelming and increase the likelihood of regret. Simplify your choices by setting clear priorities and values that guide your decision-making process. Focusing on what truly matters makes making the right choice easier and more fulfilling.

> ### Informed Decisions Lead to Greater Satisfaction

The best decisions come from a place of clarity, knowledge, and foresight. Rushing into choices without evaluating the consequences can lead to stress, regret, or unintended setbacks. Take the time to understand your options thoroughly before making decisions. You minimize regret and maximize satisfaction when you make choices based on well-researched facts, personal values, and long-term aspirations.

> ## ➤ Freedom to Choose Comes with Responsibility

The ability to choose is one of life's greatest freedoms, but it also comes with responsibility. Your choices don't just affect you; they shape your relationships, career, health, and even those around you. Being intentional with your decisions ensures you actively create the life you want rather than leaving it up to chance. Taking responsibility for your actions leads to personal growth, confidence, and a stronger sense of purpose.

> ## ➤ Your Present Choices Create Your Future Reality

Your decisions today are laying the foundation for the world you will live in tomorrow. Whether it's financial choices, career moves, or how you spend your time, each decision contributes to the life you are building. Choose wisely, think long-term, and take control of your destiny.

Final Thought

Your life is not shaped by chance but by the decisions you make every day. Be mindful, be intentional, and take responsibility for your choices. When you understand that each decision holds power, you gain the confidence to shape a future that aligns with your dreams and values.

The power to create your desired life is yours; choose wisely.

CHAPTER SEVEN

THE CYCLE OF LIFE

L ife is a voyage filled with peaks and valleys, a recurring pattern that shapes our evolution and experiences. It serves as a potent reminder that nothing in life is static and that change is an integral part of our being. By acknowledging and accepting life's cyclical nature, we can navigate its ebbs and flows with increased resilience and insight, discovering purpose and personal development.

While linear time stems from quantifying physical events, life's temporality is defined by cyclical phenomena evident in our bodily experiences. This applies to the rhythm of our heartbeat, the cycle of breathing, and the sleep pattern, among other things.

The cyclical pattern of time is tied to our continuous needs and motivates the fulfillment of our purpose. Moreover, the cyclical structure of bodily time reveals itself on a broader scale in the form of physical memory. However, this cyclical framework of experienced time conflicts with the notions of linear time, which have become more prevalent in Western cultures since the onset of the modern era.

The tension created in these instances between individuals and societal conflict can often leave us feeling anxious and burnt out. Therefore, it's important always to remind yourself that change, time, and the cycle of life are continuously happening, and allowing them to do so is vital. Life is a Cyclic Process, and Nothing Remains Constant

Life is frequently likened to an ever-revolving wheel, a metaphor that underscores its repetitive and cyclical traits. This comparison conveys that life is an endless metamorphosis, regeneration, and evolution cycle. No state is permanent; everything is fleeting and subject to alteration.

Recognizing and embracing this profound reality can be transformative and freeing, empowering us to handle life's peaks and valleys with poise and balance. Life comprises a sequence of stages that we all traverse, each presenting its distinct array of difficulties and blessings. From our first breath to our last, we constantly transition between various phases, undergoing growth, transformation, and, at times, even backsliding. This recurrent pattern is observable in numerous facets of life, from the shifting seasons to the ascension and decline of societies.

The concept of transience can be unsettling for many, as we humans often long for consistency and dread the unforeseen. However, adopting this notion can result in an extraordinary sense of liberation. By acknowledging that transformation is an inherent part of existence, we reduce our fixation on results and improve our resilience in confronting challenges.

We can learn to value elegance in each fleeting instant and experience delight in the journey rather than solely focusing on the endpoint. Acceptance serves as a robust mechanism for managing the recurrent nature of life. It does not signify inert surrender; instead, it involves recognizing reality for what it is without attempting to modify or refute it.

Once we comprehend that nothing remains unchanging, we can relinquish our opposition to change and welcome new opportunities and possibilities. This acceptance can foster enhanced flexibility, versatility, and individual development.

Our journey is punctuated by triumphant occasions and achievements, each serving as a powerful inspiration, pushing us to scale greater heights. These victories symbolize the attainment of our ambitions, the manifestation of our aspirations, and the fruits of our relentless dedication and resolve.

Such victories are significant markers that highlight our potential, pushing us forward in our quest for excellence. During such periods, we are filled with profound feelings of happiness, fulfillment, and pride. These emotions fuel our drive and reinforce our confidence in our abilities concerning future achievements.

However, it's crucial to recognize that while these moments of triumph are thrilling, they are often transient. They offer the much-needed motivation to keep striving for extraordinary feats, but they shouldn't be the solitary determinant of our self-esteem or the exclusive fountain of our joy.

In recognizing the transitory nature of these summits, we learn to value the expedition itself, deriving pleasure in the steps of progression instead of depending entirely on the result. We acquire knowledge, learn from our errors, and become more resilient through hardships. The recurrent pattern of life instructs us that failures are not everlasting. As dawn breaks after the darkest night, our existence is rejuvenated and revived.

These rejuvenation cycles empower us to discard outdated convictions, routines, and constraints, paving the way for individual development and metamorphosis.

In periods of rejuvenation, we embark on a journey of self-realization and transformation. We re-evaluate our principles, interests, and goals, consciously aligning our existence with our progressive perception of who we are. This rejuvenation stage allows us to relinquish what is no longer beneficial and seize new prospects and possibilities. Through this unending cycle of rejuvenation and rebirth, we progressively grow closer to realizing our optimal version.

As you step into the subsequent stage of your life and pledge to self-recovery, it's vital to remember that life is repetitive and ongoing. It is repetitive because it involves various cycles, some tougher than others. However, we persistently progress and develop, and each sunrise brings fresh possibilities for expansion and acknowledgment.

Existence is a give-and-take process; we are likely to receive the type of energy we radiate. This truth resembles wisdom, where the seed determines the fruit and harvest. Therefore, fostering a positive outlook is crucial to attracting the same in return. The principle of attraction should guide our daily activities and decisions. Without a positive mindset, healing becomes unattainable. The adage that we reap what we sow holds here when we commit to spreading kindness and inevitably finds its way back to us.

Change is not instantaneous; it's a gradual process that requires unwavering determination. We can successfully fend off any negative influences in our lives. This transformation can only be achieved by learning from past errors and acknowledging that such destructive patterns have ended, and we must ensure they end. And that we have firmly shut the door on this chapter. But this doesn't imply that we discard the lessons gleaned from it. To progress effectively into the new phase of our lives, we must carry these lessons, accepting our past for what it was.

One can find comfort in understanding that life is a cycle, constantly progressing and never stagnant. This signifies that we are not obliged to remain trapped or continuously revisit past traumas from which we've managed to break free. Life unfolds in phases, enabling us to mentally shut the door on a challenging phase and embark on a fresh journey. The bonds in our forged relationships tend to follow a similar cyclical pattern and phases.

The impulse to initiate a new chapter originates from within us. We possess the power to commence and conclude cycles whenever we desire. Remembering that we have autonomy over what we bring into our new phase and what we decide to leave behind is crucial.

We have the power to create ingrained in us, and with it, we make and enhance our physical and spiritual space. We also use this power to envision outcomes on our paths in a process called faith. Therefore, what we experience can be shaped and anticipated by us well in advance. When honed, the ability to envision outcomes before they materialize is an invaluable power to have. This power, also known as faith, sustains us through the undesirable parts of our path.

Moreover, recognizing that life operates on a give-and-take principle should instill a sense of hope within us. If we choose to embrace positivity, it will also be part of our lives in return. Our task is to commit ourselves to striving for betterment each day compared to the previous one, which is an ongoing process with every passing day.

As human beings, it's unrealistic to aspire to flawlessness. Nevertheless, our past shortcomings are invaluable lessons that encourage us to evolve despite them. This commitment to personal growth is one we can reaffirm each time we greet a new dawn. The mere privilege of witnessing a new day is a blessing, just as the opportunity to lead a mutually rewarding life is a treasure. In its many cycles, life is designed to offer us the opportunity to refine or correct our many experiences, perhaps through our faults.

When I wake up early to witness the sunrise, I feel a sense of physical and spiritual empowerment. I do so to welcome my day. I learned this from my father, who practiced it with the monks who taught him to pray fervently. This practice of welcoming the new day could inject motivation and a positive mindset into a depressive and unmotivated daily routine.

Start each day with affirmations of positivity and a pledge to cultivate joy. By doing so, you're fulfilling self-promises of a fresh start every day. This transformation doesn't go unnoticed; others will be inspired to emulate your positive approach. When we live this way, we become conduits of hope, and those around us reciprocate this. It's as straightforward as that.

Change is Part of Our Existence

Life often throws curveballs and hurdles that examine our fortitude and adaptability. These dips in our path could be defeats, letdowns, or unexpected barriers that upset our goals and anticipations. They can prove to be psychologically distressing and mentally demanding, compelling us to harness our latent power to endure.

Nevertheless, it's precisely during these trying periods that we frequently witness the most profound personal evolution. Amidst hardship, we acquire priceless insights into our persona and our surroundings. We cultivate tenacity, flexibility, and a knack for resolving issues.

Our encounters and experiences mold our personalities, enhance our awareness of our potential, and equip us with the fortitude to confront impending difficulties with an elevated level of self-assurance. Although stumbling blocks can initially seem disheartening and impossible, they act as catalysts for self-examination and introspection. These obstacles compel us to reassess our objectives, convictions, and approaches.

During these moments of introspection, we frequently unearth unexplored avenues, alternative viewpoints, and concealed capabilities within us. Our trials are hardships and provide the platform for self-discovery and growth. By navigating through these challenging times, we are tested and allowed to build resilience and discover ourselves in a new light.

Remaining Inspired

I pledged myself to a lifetime of continuous learning when I chose to enter healthcare. Where most occupations find a surge in demand thrilling, the perspective in the medical field is strikingly different.

The emergence of disease, rather than serving as a source of inspiration, often evokes a melancholy mood, particularly when contemplating preventable diseases that could have been avoided with correct policy decisions and appropriate resource distribution.

For example, recent political instability in Sub-Saharan Africa has led to living conditions adverse to health. Although conflict might spur growth in specific sectors, it typically results in an unnecessary escalation in death and suffering.

Like numerous benevolent healthcare practitioners, I am motivated by illness and hardship.

We work diligently to explore the fundamental issues and conceive strategies to ease distress. I must extend my reading scope beyond medical boundaries and interact with specialists from various disciplines.

A rudimentary comprehension of diverse professions is vital if we are to utilize their skills effectively in tackling the urgent problems faced by our communities. I believe that the true worth of our existence is appreciated when we fulfill our life's mission. The satisfaction I derive from assisting a patient or averting an ailment via enlightened decisions fuels my motivation, fortifying my commitment to this honorable vocation despite the daily hurdles encountered.

Embrace Change and Growth

> **Recognize Life's Cycles to Build Resilience**

Life is filled with peaks and valleys, joys and hardships. Recognizing that every phase is temporary helps you navigate challenges and triumphs more easily. Understanding that nothing remains the same forever allows you to appreciate the good times and endure the difficult ones with patience and wisdom.

> ### Embrace Change as a Natural Part of Life

As seasons shift, so do our experiences, emotions, and circumstances. Holding on too tightly to a single phase can lead to frustration while embracing the natural flow of life fosters growth and adaptability. Every challenge brings an opportunity for renewal, and every joy is meant to be fully lived in the present.

> ### Find Liberation in Life's Transience

Accepting that everything changes, from relationships to career paths to personal identities, can be unsettling and liberating. When you stop resisting change, you free yourself from unnecessary fear and learn to appreciate each moment for what it is. The beauty of life lies in its impermanence, making every experience unique and meaningful.

> ➢ **Appreciate the Repetitive Yet Transformative Nature of Life**

Life is often described as a wheel, cycling through success, failure, growth, and renewal phases. While certain themes may reappear throughout your life, each new cycle offers deeper insight and a fresh perspective. Learning from these repetitions helps you evolve rather than repeat past mistakes.

> ➢ **Allow Renewal and Growth to Shape Your Path**

Every stage of life presents an opportunity for reinvention. Whether shedding outdated beliefs, adopting new perspectives, or stepping into a new phase of personal development, you can embrace transformation. Just as nature continuously renews itself, so can you refresh your mindset, ambitions, and approach to life.

> ➢ **Understand Life's Give-and-Take Principle**

Life operates on an exchange; what you give often returns in some form. Whether through kindness, effort, or learning, each day is a chance to invest in your future self. Make conscious choices to add positivity, wisdom, and purpose to your life and the lives of others, and you contribute to a meaningful cycle of growth and fulfillment.

> **Use Life's Cycles as a Guide to Personal Evolution**

Rather than resisting life's inevitable changes, view them as invitations for self-discovery. You become more adaptable and at peace when you align yourself with life's natural rhythms of rest and action, challenge and ease, endings and new beginnings.

Final Thought

Life is not a straight path but a series of evolving cycles that invite you to grow, change, and discover new depths within yourself. Instead of resisting its flow, embrace each phase with an open heart and a curious mind.

When you understand and accept the cycle of life, you stop fearing change and start embracing every experience as an opportunity for transformation.

CHAPTER EIGHT

EMPOWERMENT THROUGH GOALS

Becoming empowered is a voyage, a path to self-realization and development. It is understood that we have the potential and power to mold one's future. One of the fundamental milestones in this voyage is establishing and documenting objectives. Objectives offer a nautical chart to your success, steering you towards your destination.

They serve as a linkage between your ambitions and reality, converting vague dreams into concrete aims. This chapter aims to empower and navigate you through establishing objectives, implementing actions, and seeking advice when uncertain.

How often have you established an objective and made a few strides towards it, only to abandon it because you thought it was too challenging? How many goals have you established and not pursued to completion at all?

Objectives serve as a vital catalyst propelling us towards fulfillment and attainment, yet many stumble on this path. However, those who persist and realize their objectives invariably positively influence their lives and are self-motivated in future undertakings.

Empowerment is "the bestowed authority or capacity to carry out a task" and "the journey of growing stronger and more self-assured, particularly in governing one's existence and asserting one's entitlements."

Thus, empowered individuals have granted themselves the "authority" to pursue their aspirations or transform into the person they envision. They've cultivated resilience and confidence by consciously directing their actions and choices instead of permitting external influences or situations to dominate them.

The Importance of Goal Setting

In our current world, establishing objectives is constantly underscored by inspirational orators, self-improvement literature, and many success narratives. Setting goals has become a preferred method for realizing one's dreams, from personal growth to professional progression.

Nevertheless, even as we frequently encounter stress and doubt about the criticality of goal setting, it's not uncommon to question whether it's merely a fashionable catchphrase or possesses genuine worth.

Is a clear goal essential to secure what we desire in life? In other words, can we begin the journey and arrive at the intended destination without prior planning, directions, or ensuring adequate resources for the endeavor?

To comprehend the importance of setting goals, ponder how it can influence results in these four distinct ways:

Selection

Establishing objectives profoundly affects results by directing your focus and efforts towards activities that align with your goals while steering you away from actions that do not contribute to them. This process increases your decisiveness in your actions, as you tend to concentrate on those with the highest probability of assisting you in attaining your goals.

Selection also helps us assemble the team required to achieve the desired goal. I can say with certainty that selection will determine whose companionship you may accept or deny as you focus on accomplishing your goal.

Exertion

Objectives can inspire you to exert more effort than usual. This heightened level of exertion could be attributed to your aspiration to realize the intended result and the perceived value of achieving that goal. It is well known in the faith community that a written goal increases one's belief in its achievement.

Tenacity

Objectives can also impact results by amplifying your readiness to remain steadfast despite obstacles. When hurdles, setbacks, or difficulties present themselves, keeping a specific objective in mind can bolster your motivation and resilience.

Thought Process

Setting a goal promotes deeper contemplation about one's behavior, habits, and the actions required to realize the intended outcome. This introspection can induce behavioral shifts, such as incorporating new habits or routines to accomplish the objective.

I lived with my friend's family (Hope) during my first and second years in college. His uncle (Ni Joe) would emphasize goal setting. He often said that setting goals and writing them down forces us to behave differently.

As a young man, I wrote down my lifetime goal to become a medical doctor, and that forced me to avoid every situation that could jeopardize my chances of being accepted into medical school. I spent most of my time in the library studying and getting out of trouble with the law. Ni Joe deeply embedded in me that a clean background check and an excellent grade point average (GPA) are mandatory for medical school admissions.

Setting goals enables you to assign importance to your tasks and concentrate your resources on what truly matters. It steers your focus away from activities that don't contribute to your goals and towards those that do. This strategic approach enhances the utilization of your time and resources, thereby escalating your probability of triumph.

Consider, for instance, an individual aiming to shed some pounds. Their attention would be concentrated on consuming nutritious food and maintaining a regular physical activity routine while consciously evading habits that could obstruct their advancement, such as indulging in high-calorie edibles or leading a sedentary lifestyle.

Establishing objectives is a potent instrument for individual progression and enhancement. It signifies the preliminary move to make the unseen seen and the intangible materialize. Objectives instill direction in our lives, imbue them with purpose, and offer a sense of accomplishment. They serve as a gauge for our aspirations and a tool to track our advancement.

Objectives are the tangible realizations of our wishes, converted into actionable targets. They segment our aspirations of attainable endeavors into smaller, more manageable undertakings. Our objectives could be diverse, from career progression to reaching a specific educational attainment to bettering our health or cultivating relationships. Without goals, our desires remain theoretical, our dreams continue to be dreams, and our actions are devoid of guidance. Goals bestow upon us a sense of purpose and path. They invigorate our motivation and delineate a route towards our coveted destination.

Setting objectives functions similarly to a roadmap. It gives you a clear direction, instilling excitement, dedication, vitality, and a purpose to rise daily. It brings about a sense of liveliness in you. When your path is defined, your life experiences less pressure and tension since you know your destination.

It's comparable to possessing a map that points out your course. You refrain from wasting time moving aimlessly and reaching nowhere. Having an objective makes you feel like you are progressing towards a significant endpoint, enhancing feelings of happiness, security, strength, and confidence.

When you establish a goal, you concentrate on a specific objective, preventing you from squandering your resources on every opportunity. The absence of a goal may lead you to initiate a task only to shift onto another before its completion. If this pattern continues and you never end what you started, the chances of achieving something meaningful are slim.

The act of setting an objective and striving to fulfill it brings about feelings of hope, tranquility within oneself, and self-assuredness. It is akin to illuminating a flashlight that brightens your path and assists you in progressing linearly rather than moving in circles.

Embrace the process as you work towards your objectives. While your aim is crucial, the path that leads you there is equally paramount. This journey provides opportunities to acquire new knowledge, encounter unique and thrilling experiences, engage with different personalities, and develop novel abilities.

Think of it as a train ride to a specific location. You could spend the entire trip anxiously, continually glancing at your timepiece and restlessly anticipating your arrival. Alternatively, you could appreciate the ride, take in the beautiful landscape, delve into a good book, or even build friendships with fellow passengers.

If you learn to relish the path rather than eagerly anticipate reaching your destination, you'll find greater joy and satisfaction. Adopting this perspective while pursuing your objectives can foster an enhanced sense of happiness.

While your goal determines your direction, all the steps leading to its realization, including the creative thinking process, the actions taken, and the rewards gained, are meant to be savored.

The journey can be lengthened, and the actual moment of arrival may be fleeting. So, why not make the most of the journey instead of impatiently yearning for the endpoint? After all, the value of our goals is inherently tied to the experiences amassed and lessons learned on the way there.

When one shares the lessons concerning their achievements, the journey or process to these goals is shared, not the endpoint itself. Therefore, concerning goals and their accomplishment, the lessons to be shared and the stories to be told are not at the end but rather in the journey from conception to fruition of the objective.

You now understand the importance of setting goals and striving towards their achievement. Thus, it's time to derive pleasure from every instant spent pursuing your objectives. Integrate elements of amusement and delight into your process, and you'll notice how your life reflects these same qualities.

The Importance of Action in Achieving Desired Outcomes

Establishing objectives is a crucial initial phase, yet it's inadequate in isolation. Objectives without pursuits are merely dreams. Action is the conduit that connects our ambitions to their realization.

Actions embody our dedication toward the accomplishment of our aspirations. Once we've established our objectives, the subsequent step involves formulating an action strategy. This plan functions as a roadmap, outlining the measures we must implement to realize our aspirations. Additionally, it equips us to foresee challenges and construct strategies to surmount them.

Implementing action can be daunting. It frequently necessitates venturing outside our familiar territory, experimenting with new concepts, and risking setbacks. However, action is indispensable for development and advancement. Through actions, we acquire knowledge, surmount hurdles, and ultimately fulfill our ambitions.

Suppose you are conceiving a concept, aspiration, or goal. In that case, it is perfectly fine to let it mature, stew, and develop in your thoughts for an adequate period akin to an infant's gestation period. However, there comes a stage when it's necessary to birth this 'concept' and offer it an opportunity to evolve and thrive in the tangible world.

Like a nurturing mother who dutifully looks after her newborn until it reaches adulthood, you will cultivate and care for your freshly generated idea, nourishing it daily and administering tender sustenance and assistance one day at a time. There will be happiness, initial troubles, minor setbacks, illness, and recovery along the journey, but this is an inherent part of the process.

As your concept, aspiration, or vision matures, transitioning from infancy to adolescence and adulthood, you will retrospect with a sense of accomplishment.

The key to attaining success is taking the initiative to act. It's a straightforward reality that dreams, visions, and targets can only materialize through proactive actions. No number of well-crafted theories and strategic plans will have any impact if you fail to take the necessary steps towards action.

Envision, consider, design a plan around it, and then put it into motion. Pursue it relentlessly. Implement your plans. The ability to execute an idea effectively differentiates individuals, even when their ideas might be similar. The initial step is often the most daunting part of any journey. Frequently, individuals are uncertain about the ideal path to follow to realize their dreams. So, they find themselves waiting for all the puzzle pieces to fall into place or for the perfect moment to commence their journey.

It becomes a game of patience, waiting for all the jigsaw components to align and create an understandable picture, anticipating the right scenarios and situations. It involves a continuous cycle of delaying tasks, an infestation of postponements, overthinking, and the perpetual "I will do it someday" promise.

But what's the strategy for initiating action? At what percentage of resources should action begin? Start with whatever key components are available and add as you go without fearing failure, remaining focused on the goal and strategy. The initial step may be daunting, but it is necessary.

Action is essential to making any headway. Consider all the positive results and potentialities you aspire to; this should motivate you to embark on your journey. Remember that countless others have been in your current position, and they have found the courage to leap into action.

Begin at your current level, then gradually enhance your abilities and productivity. Do something. Inactivity is a dream destroyer. The harsh truth is that if you don't make a move to chase your aspirations, nobody else will do it on your behalf. The impact of a goal begins with your first action toward achieving it. Goals by themselves, unachieved, have no effect.

Action gives life to ideas.

Even a vehicle remains stationary until some action is taken, such as pressing the start button, igniting the engine, or instructing the car to commence operations (as seen in some contemporary models). The crux here is the necessity of action. It's essential to implement your thoughts to bring them into existence.

Action gives rise to momentum. The higher an aircraft's altitude, the less power it consumes, enabling it to maintain stability over extended durations and, thus, reach its destination more swiftly. However, it took much energy and coordination to attain this height from its initial position of rest.

When you act, you accomplish tasks. Yet, the journey may not always be smooth. You may encounter obstacles and make errors along the path. However, having a clear vision of your end goal is crucial. As you persistently forge ahead and make concentrated strides toward your success, maintain this image.

When in Doubt, Seek Counsel

As we strive to achieve our objectives, we are bound to confront various challenges and uncertainties. These could stem from internal elements such as anxiety about failing, fear due to past failed attempts, or external factors like criticism or lack of moral support. In these situations, obtaining guidance can be helpful.

Obtaining guidance entails reaching out to others for counsel, direction, or support. This could be a mentor, a coach, a reliable friend, or a family member.

These individuals can offer reassurance or valuable wisdom, viewpoints, or solutions that might not have crossed our minds.

Contrary to common belief, seeking advice does not signal a deficiency but indicates prudence. It exhibits humility, a readiness to acquire knowledge, and a receptiveness to constructive criticism. It is an essential instrument for personal development and can substantially improve our possibilities of realizing our aspirations.

Self-empowerment through goal setting is a transformative journey of self-exploration and development. It involves establishing objectives, initiating steps toward their completion, and seeking advice when uncertain. This methodology allows us to mold our future, unlock our capabilities, and fulfill our ambitions.

Remember, the expedition of countless miles commences with a singular move. Begin outlining your objectives today, act upon them, and never hesitate to consult for advice when uncertainties arise.

Achieving empowerment is within your grasp. You possess the ability to sculpt your future. Have faith in your abilities, outline your objectives, initiate steps towards them, and you are bound to attain the results you desire. Remember that past successes or failures do not guarantee future outcomes; every attempt to achieve a goal is unique.

Own Your Future

> ➤ **Recognizing Your Power to Shape Your Future**

The most profound form of empowerment comes from acknowledging that you can define your path. Setting clear and intentional goals allows you to take control of your life's direction, ensuring that you are actively shaping your future rather than being shaped by circumstances.

➢ **Goals Are More Than Aspirations—They Are Tools for Success**

Goals are not just wishful thinking; they are structured pathways toward fulfillment and achievement. Whether in your career, relationships, health, or personal growth, setting specific, actionable goals provides clarity and motivation to move forward with purpose.

➢ **A Well-Defined Plan Transforms Goals into Reality**

Having a vision is essential, but it remains an idea without a plan. A clear roadmap outlining the necessary steps bridges the gap between ambition and achievement. Breaking goals into smaller, manageable steps makes them less overwhelming and more attainable, allowing for steady and measurable progress.

> ➤ **Challenges Are Inevitable, but Resilience Is Key**

The path to achieving goals is not always smooth; doubts, setbacks, and external pressures are part of the process. Rather than viewing these obstacles as deterrents, they see them as opportunities for growth. Every challenge you face refines your resilience and deepens your commitment to your aspirations.

> ➤ **Seeking Guidance Strengthens Your Progress**

No one succeeds in isolation. Mentors, coaches, and supportive friends provide invaluable insights, encouragement, and fresh perspectives when obstacles arise. Reaching out for guidance is not a sign of weakness but a strategy for accelerated growth.

Learning from those who have walked similar paths can shorten your learning curve and enhance your confidence.

> ➤ **Goal Setting Fuels Continuous Learning and Adaptation**

Setting and pursuing goals is a dynamic process that encourages constant self-improvement. The journey itself is just as important as reaching the destination, as it cultivates discipline, adaptability, and a mindset of lifelong learning.

> ➤ **Each Step Forward Builds Confidence and Momentum**

The act of working toward a goal is empowering in itself. Each milestone reached reinforces your belief in your abilities, making you more confident in tackling future challenges. No matter how small, progress compounds over time, bringing you closer to the life you envision.

Final Thought

Empowerment through goal setting is about taking ownership of your choices, building resilience, and committing yourself to personal growth. Your future is shaped by your actions today.

Start now by defining your goals, acting, and trusting in your ability to achieve them. The power to succeed is already within you.

CHAPTER NINE

HUMILITY AT HEART

It's a prevalent misunderstanding in leadership that exceptional leaders exhibit unwavering self-assurance and unshakeable trust in their capabilities. Authentic leadership stretches beyond self-confidence and surpasses the self. Outstanding leaders appreciate that they don't possess all the solutions, and their power is rooted in their capability to acquire knowledge from others.

I have traveled widely, immersed myself in other cultures, and experienced different leadership approaches. However, across these cultures, I have noticed that result is the focus of measure of leadership efficiency. To this, I resolved that to be effective, leaders mustn't be the most intelligent or resourceful members of their team. They, however, must be effective communicators who can bring out the best in others and coordinate the efforts of their teammates such that the goal is achieved. To remain competitive, though, influential leaders must seek to improve themselves and their teams daily.

In this chapter, we'll examine the significance of humility in leadership and as individuals. We'll also investigate how accepting mistakes and fostering a genuine yearning to learn can uplift and inspire.

At the core of humility lies a preparedness to recognize one's limitations and vulnerabilities. This is positive when you acknowledge that you are not without flaws and that your comprehension and proficiency have limitations. You can cultivate an ambiance that encourages teamwork, transparency, and psychological safety by espousing humility.

You welcome a variety of viewpoints, appreciate the input of others, and foster a culture of perpetual learning. Humility leads to approachability and breaks down the barriers that impede effective communication between leaders and their teams.

Live Life with Humility

As a medical professional, my story is primarily shaped by my engagements with those I treat. I've discovered that the essence of providing medical care is rooted in the bond that forms between me and the individual I'm treating. This mutual relationship is built on a foundation of trust and comprehension, and it is surprisingly unaffected by the prestige of my alma mater or the extent of my achievements.

From the perspective of those under my care, my qualifications are peripheral. Their primary focus is on an uncomplicated yet deeply significant question: Can

I aid them in their hour of need? To effectively convey my ability to assist, it's crucial that I first nurture a strong connection with them. This entails recognizing them as more than just their health issue, recalling personal aspects about them, and persistently recognizing these non-medical details every time we converse.

This habit gives them a subtle reassurance that my concern extends to them as individuals, not merely as patients. Therefore, an interaction, for example, with John, the 50-year-old father who happens to be living with diabetes, is focused more on his social person than just his health condition.

To help John build trust in the fact that I genuinely *care* about him and can deliver healthcare, I tend to learn, share, and remember his job, children, spouse, pets, interests, and so on. Patients are like friends; you only see them when they need you.

Establishing a relationship that encourages the patient to willingly share the necessary information for their treatment pivots on the axis of humility. This attribute may not always be inherently present but can be cultivated and honed.

The essence of this practice revolves around putting the patient's needs above mine. At that moment, within the clinical environment of the consultation room, the focus is solely on the patient and their immediate circumstances.

This methodology, in response, fosters a unique spiritual link, often called rapport. This rapport is not a spontaneous incident; it's a repetitive result when humility is in action. It's a bond that goes beyond the fundamental doctor-patient relationship, shaping an environment conducive to healing. Rapport is the foundation and the beginning of a great patient-doctor relationship.

As a physician, I've embraced the virtue of modesty, which has helped me understand my vocation fully. I've come to accept that despite my medical education, my patients enlighten me daily on the true essence of providing healthcare. This tale of modesty in inpatient treatment doesn't just belong to me; it echoes the experiences of each medical professional who has gained the ability to perceive their patients beyond their ailments. It's a narrative of comprehension, rapport, and therapeutic recovery.

In business, humility is an essential element. It acknowledges the intrinsic value of others and creates an environment that promotes reciprocal respect and comprehension. This fundamental truth applies to every aspect of life, encompassing health services and business operations.

As a medical practitioner, it is crucial to realize that the core of patient treatment is rooted in your ability to create a robust connection with them, seeing them beyond their afflictions. Similarly, for a business professional, it is vital to understand that the heart of a thriving enterprise does not solely lie in the commodities or services offered but also in the bonds nurtured. With this bond, the clientele believes that you, the business, genuinely care about the problem your product or services are meant to solve.

Within the commerce domain, a consumer is not merely a number to augment earnings but a person who places great value on respect and honor. In aggressive commercial environments, the secret to flourishing lies in offering an exceptional product or service and forging enduring consumer relationships. Just as a patient looks for a doctor who can empathize with their condition, a consumer seeks a business that understands and appreciates their distinct needs and desires.

When there is a mutually beneficial exchange in value during a business interaction, the phrase, "It was nice doing business with you" is usually exchanged. This statement is a testament to the fact that the value in business interactions goes beyond exchanging goods and services for money. It matters what kind of experience these interactions lead to. Whether it felt nice or not does matter to all parties involved. This is true in everyday commerce as it is in the business of medicine, mainly the doctor-patient interaction.

Therefore, modesty becomes an essential factor in commercial interactions. It's not merely about being agreeable; it's about exhibiting regard for the customer's principles and necessities, welcoming feedback, and persistently pursuing enhancement. Modesty enables one to comprehend that the value transacted in a business deal is multi-dimensional. It's not solely about the product or its cost but also the experience, the relationship, and the mutual respect between the purchaser and the vendor.

Consequently, modesty serves a dual purpose: It is a requirement for agreeability and a vital element in crafting a delightful business engagement. By placing the customer's needs and experiences above their own, business proprietors can nurture a devoted customer base that continues to return because they feel appreciated and esteemed.

Modesty enables physicians to regard their patients as mentors, and entrepreneurs perceive their clients as collaborators. This change in viewpoint cultivates a relationship that goes beyond the mere exchange of services, forging an environment conducive to development, knowledge acquisition, and reciprocal esteem.

How, you ask, can a patient serve as a mentor, a mentor being an experienced and trusted adviser? Well, consider who could be trusted to have experience with the disease, and think about how the disease influences the knowledge you seek as you learn more to help the patient. Patients, therefore, qualify to mentor their healthcare providers. They have the disease and hence the experience that comes with it. To learn about the disease, the doctor needs the patient's experience. Therefore, the patient, being a source of knowledge concerning the disease, becomes a mentor.

How Humility Enhances the Power of Choice

Humility, an enduring quality echoed across generations, continues to be a foundational element of human nature and communication. It is a principle deeply embedded in our past, traditions, and mental processes, providing a significant understanding of humanity's essence.

Humility is an influential characteristic that remarkably intensifies decision-making power, particularly in sectors like healthcare and business.

Professionals who recognize and incorporate humility can make more informed and empathetic decisions. Humility enables individuals to acknowledge their constraints and preconceptions, promoting introspection and continuous learning. By doing this, they can better understand patients' or consumers' beliefs, values, and requirements. This is crucial in making decisions that respect and prioritize these individuals' experiences.

Indeed, humility plays a crucial role in tackling power imbalances. Taking healthcare as a case study, physicians who embody humility tend to view their patients as collaborators in the healing process, empowering them with control and options. Such practices lead to patient autonomy in healthcare.

In business, humility enables leaders to attune their ears to the voices of their team members and clientele, paving the way for more encompassing and client-oriented decisions. Products and services designed with the client in mind tend to be most successful.

Additionally, humility creates an atmosphere conducive to open conversations and mutual regard.

This fosters more balanced decision-making processes, granting equal importance to diverse viewpoints and experiences. Therefore, humility amplifies the potency of choice and elevates the caliber of those choices. The decisions become more inclusive, empathetic, and focused on the patient's or customer's needs.

This process cultivates fresh insights and fosters newfound skills. The principle is simple: the individual filled with pride will leave with lesser gains than the modest individual seeking knowledge. Pride, the opposing force to humility, is quite an impediment to improvement.

Aristotle said, "We believe good-hearted people to a greater extent and more quickly than others on all subjects in general and completely so in cases where there is not exact knowledge but room for doubt. Character is almost, so to speak, the controlling factor in persuasion."

Reflecting on this quote, I concluded that those who present good character during interactions will gain trust even quicker. This is important, especially in healthcare, where interactions require time-sensitive actions.

The Role of Humility in Seeking and Accepting Help

Humility serves as a crucial factor in soliciting and embracing support from others. Initially, it enables individuals to acknowledge their constraints and the reality that they don't possess all the solutions. This introspective realization is the inaugural move towards extending a hand for help and welcoming aid from others.

When I moved to the U.S., one of the cultural shocks I experienced was the hesitancy to accept help when they genuinely needed it. In most cultures I have interacted with, it is widely understood and even encouraged that when one is seen to be in need, help should be offered immediately.

However, in the U.S., I've heard on several occasions those who fall and struggle to get up say, "I am okay," and will not take the hand that was extended to help raise them back up. Help, if taken habitually, may imply a fault in our productivity; however, when taken occasionally, it could be the lifeline we need to stay afloat and strategize.

In addition, humility cultivates an aura of receptiveness and esteem for others' abilities, wisdom, and life experiences. It motivates individuals to appreciate others' contributions and contemplate their viewpoints or resolutions, which could potentially be more efficient or inventive.

Humility fosters a climate of reciprocal respect and teamwork. When people display humility, they are more inclined to listen, comprehend, and value the help offered by their peers. Their defenses are lowered, and they become more open to fresh perspectives or constructive feedback, promoting personal and occupational development. To facilitate this, we need to look at humility in a broader context:

Humility in Leadership

The concept of humility in leadership signals a transformation into leadership models. Leadership is no longer purely about command and dominance; it's about guiding with a mindset of modesty. Leaders who embody humility actively listen, empower their groups, and recognize their flaws. Their professional yet compassionate way of steering cultivates a positive workplace environment and inspires others to adopt a similar humble attitude.

Humility in Intellect

Intellectual modesty, a significant aspect of this virtue, inspires people to seek knowledge with an unbiased mindset. It requires recognition of one's cognitive constraints and the potential for error. In an era where information is abundant and continually shifting, fostering intellectual modesty becomes crucial for individual and communal development.

Humility in Culture

Cultural modesty, another aspect of this complex idea, involves appreciating and honoring various cultures and viewpoints. It encourages individuals to demonstrate a caring and empathetic approach towards those from diverse backgrounds.

In our progressively interconnected world, cultural modesty fosters unity and comprehension among individuals with differing beliefs and customs. Cultural humility doesn't diminish one's esteem for a culture. It helps us celebrate our culture alongside others.

When I was in medical school, I remember a new and expensive student lounge being created, and we would often sit for lunch with classmates and chitchat about what was new.

One such day, a classmate brought a meal celebrating her culture. When she took it out of the microwave, she made an apologetic disclaimer about the "acquired" aroma from her meal.

I remember telling her not to apologize for celebrating her heritage with food, no matter what others judged the aroma. We must distinguish cultural humility from humiliation, shame, or inadequacy in oneself.

Because of cultural humility, interpreters are provided for those who need them, and printed materials are made in multiple languages to serve a multilingual population. In medicine, developing treatment plans that consider patients' religious beliefs is an act attributed to cultural humility.

Humility is a virtue that should be treasured, yet it's crucial to differentiate between genuine humility and its counterfeit counterpart. Genuine humility springs from a sincere understanding of oneself and an appreciation for others. On the other hand, pseudo-humility can mask a lack of sincerity, making it critical to distinguish between the two for self-improvement and the fostering of positive interpersonal connections.

When we investigate the multifaceted nature of humility, we find that it spans a variety of attitudes and conducts. From intellectual humility to cultural humility and even humility in leadership, each facet uniquely contributes to enhancing comprehension and individual development.

Adopting a modest way of life begins with fostering an attitude of humility. It revolves around acknowledging that we are merely minute participants in the vast panorama of life. This viewpoint promotes gratitude for our existing blessings rather than perpetually striving for more.

Modesty is not a passive state but an active endeavor. It encompasses respecting others, being a good listener, and appreciating their viewpoints. It implies accepting our errors and gaining wisdom from them. Implementing modesty in everyday life results in deeper relationships and significant personal development.

Modesty provides balance and clarity. It equips us to handle difficulties with elegance and tenacity. We become more flexible and receptive to fresh ideas and outlooks by welcoming modesty.

Lead With Humility at Heart

Humility is a fundamental aspect of both leadership and personal growth. It involves acknowledging that you do not possess all the answers, and that true strength often comes from your capacity to learn from others. Here are some valuable lessons on humility:

> ➤ **Humility is the Foundation of Growth and Leadership**
>
> True leadership is not about having all the answers; it's about creating an environment where learning and collaboration thrive. Acknowledging that others have

valuable insights and skills enhances teamwork, communication, and effectiveness. Growth begins when you stay open to learning from those around you.

> ➤ **Trust os Built Through Genuine Connection**

Whether in business, healthcare, or leadership, your ability to connect with others determines your effectiveness. Patients, customers, and team members respond more positively when they feel seen, heard, and respected.

Humility fosters trust by ensuring that people feel valued as clients, colleagues, and individuals with unique experiences and perspectives.

Great Leaders Listen More Than They Speak

Humility strengthens decision-making by encouraging inclusivity and empathy. When you acknowledge that you don't have all the answers, you become more receptive to new ideas, allowing you to make better, more well-rounded decisions. In fields where the well-being of others is at stake, such as healthcare and business, humility ensures that choices reflect the needs of those affected.

Your Customers Are Not Just Transactions: They Are Relationships

In business, humility means recognizing that success isn't just about profit; it's about people. Prioritizing customer experiences, valuing feedback, and respecting their needs create stronger relationships and long-term loyalty. Shifting the focus from "What can I sell?" to "How can I serve?" businesses cultivate deeper trust and sustained success.

> ➢ **Seeking Help Is a Strength, not a Weakness**

The most effective individuals are not those who try to do everything alone but those who recognize when to seek support. Asking for guidance, mentorship, or collaboration demonstrates self-awareness and wisdom. Humility allows you to embrace the knowledge and skills of others, making you more adaptable and effective in any field.

> ## Humility Fosters Respect and Teamwork

A humble leader uplifts those around them, creating a workplace culture where everyone feels valued. When people feel heard and respected, they are more motivated to contribute their best work. Humility fosters collaboration, improves morale, and strengthens team dynamics, leading to better outcomes and a more positive work environment.

> ## Humility Enhances Impact Without Diminishing Self-Worth

Being humble doesn't mean downplaying your abilities or achievements. Instead, it means understanding your role in a larger mission and respecting the contributions of others.

Integrating humility into daily practices deepens relationships, improves leadership, and creates more meaningful, lasting impacts in both personal and professional spheres.

Final Thought

Humility is not a weakness but a quiet strength that leads to deeper connections, smarter decisions, and greater impact. When you lead with humility, you build trust, inspire collaboration, and create space for growth for yourself and those around you.

True leadership begins with humility. Embrace, practice, and watch its power unfold in your life.

CHAPTER TEN

THE IMPACT OF ACTIONS

Initiating action is the ignition spark that propels transformation, and when this action is imbued with optimism, it heralds constructive metamorphoses. This is an unequivocal invitation to leaders from all fields and at every administration level to leverage their distinct capabilities and influence to deliver unmatched service to their societies.

Evaluating one's contribution to society is undeniably tied to one's persistent chase for perfection, a journey that necessitates incessantly exploring inventive methods to augment and polish one's service.

Should the standard of your service remain unchanged, mirroring the same criteria as it did six months ago, then regrettably, it has now descended into the realm of commonplace, and you have stopped growing.

Every leader is thus faced with a task - to dedicate their energy and assets towards fostering the future generation, readying them to take on the leadership role. Absent a group of individuals who exhibit an equal degree of brilliance in delivering services, actual growth or enlargement is unattainable.

Consequently, a leader who does not lay the groundwork for the succeeding generation has not fulfilled their obligation. Developing a fresh batch of extraordinary leaders is essential to successful leadership.

The idea of developing the next generation of leaders begs the following questions:

✓ How come some organizations thrive with the same leadership, lasting more than one generational gap?

✓ How can they consolidate and harness these differences to achieve the desired result?

✓ Is change in leadership a necessity for growth?

✓ Are we searching for new people, ideas/processes, or both?

To answer these questions, we must attempt to define who a leader is within the context of an organization.

Leadership is anyone whose function can influence the organization's results. Therefore, it is more of a role than a position. The amount of responsibility an individual takes reflects their level of influence and, hence, the hierarchy. This approach to leadership is

194

seen in the core values of organizations such as Amazon and Apple.

When employees are told they are leaders, they treat the organization as an owner, which translates into positive productivity. Therefore, a new generation of leaders applies to all levels of responsibility within an organization. New leadership is a broad statement that includes changes in people, responsibility, ideas, processes, organizational core values, etc.

Some leading organizations use client feedback to know when leadership change is necessary. By client feedback, I mean the competitiveness of their goods and services in the marketplace. Therefore, at every level of leadership, if an individual isn't training someone to take over from them, then they, without knowing, are being complacent.

Suppose growth is the target for an organization. In that case, every leader should search for newer responsibilities to grow into while delegating some tasks (training) to those who will take their current responsibility as they advance. Concerning generational gaps, in which the differences in opinions and outlooks between one generation and another lie, organizations with teams representing the clientele demographic have the advantage! How so? You may ask.

Consider a company that produces beachwear. Keep in mind the age demographic that often goes to the beach. Say that older creative design team members whose creations were successful in the 1990s and early 2000s are maintained.

To be successful in today's marketplace, this creative team could use the ideas of the current demographic of beachwear clients. There's a rule of thumb in design: let those who use it help design it. It is exemplary leadership practice to provide leadership changes that benefit the client.

Act Intentionally

Recognizing the significance of deliberate actions is essential for individual and career growth. It enables us to coordinate our choices with our principles, objectives, and dreams, resulting in more rewarding and significant outcomes.

Deliberate actions refer to those that are pondered and purposefully selected. They demand a lucid understanding of what we aim to accomplish and the reasons behind it. This clear understanding steers us in identifying the most suitable strategies to attain our goals.

When we deliberate our actions, we are more prone to remain concentrated and dedicated to our duties. We are not simply responding to situations or going through the motions but actively molding our journey. This forward-thinking approach can enhance efficiency, gratification, and triumph in various facets of life.

Moreover, deliberate actions assist us in avoiding remorse and guilt. Purposefully deciding our course of action can prevent hasty decisions leading to future regret. Assuming responsibility for our actions promotes a feeling of liability and progress.

I have an experience that occurs every time I give a keynote address; often, after my talks, I am approached by a large portion of the audience, some of whom are so patient as they prefer not just to meet and greet briefly. Still, instead, they want to have a conversation. I usually would make an appointment with them so I could at least meet all those in line. During these brief introductions, individuals would reiterate a particular message in the talk and explain how it relates to them.

At this time, they would share a plan or dream and how my talk awakened their passion for the subject matter. My response is usually as follows; "ma'am/sir, plans and goals without action are merely for entertainment purposes; they help to prevent the awkward silence at the dinner table." This reply, which may appear rude to a bystander, is given to provoke action.

If everyone who plans and sets goals could proceed to act, we would see more advancement in our society than we could imagine. Action in the right direction is what completes a goal. Act and watch what happens next.

In the larger framework of society, actions driven by good intentions can significantly contribute to societal transformation. When a clear purpose guides our actions, we tend to evaluate the broader implications of our decisions, resulting in choices grounded in ethics and sustainability.

Every Outcome is a Result of Choice or Action

The consequences we encounter in our existence directly stem from the decisions we make and the actions we take. This fundamental yet deeply insightful understanding is critical to grasping the significant influence of our deeds. It emphasizes the ideology that we're not merely bystanders in life's play but proactive participants sculpting our fate.

Our actions physically embody our decision-making process, a tangible representation of our thoughts and convictions. Our actions are our thoughts manifested. They are the means through which we bring our ideas and plans to life, converting them from theoretical notions into practical results. When we decide to act, we initiate a chain of events, each with significance.

The repercussions of our immediate or long-term deeds can profoundly affect our lives, the people around us, and society. When we decide to act, we indirectly select the consequences we desire or are prepared to endure. That's not to suggest that we can foresee or regulate all outcomes, but it is within our power to sway them via our decisions and actions.

Comprehending our actions' ramifications is crucial to personal and professional growth. It gives us the power to take control of our lives, make enlightened choices, and act with deliberate intent. Furthermore, it instills a sense of responsibility, inspiring us to own up to our actions and their subsequent effects.

Empowerment Through Optimistic Action

Optimism is a "feeling-good" emotion and a driving force for effective action. When leaders approach their tasks and challenges positively, they are more likely to inspire confidence and enthusiasm in others. This optimism fosters an environment where creativity and innovation can thrive, as people feel more empowered to think outside the box and propose novel solutions.

Empowerment through action underscores that real change occurs when thoughts and plans are put into motion. The steps taken, decisions, and strategies implemented translate visionary ideas into tangible results. This process requires leaders to be visionaries and doers willing to roll up their sleeves and get involved in making things happen.

Moreover, optimistic action is about leveraging one's unique abilities for the greater good. Each leader brings a distinct set of skills, experiences, and perspectives. Combined with a positive and proactive approach, the potential for making a meaningful impact is greatly amplified. Leaders are thus encouraged to recognize and harness their unique strengths, channeling them into actions that contribute positively to their communities or organizations.

This is more than maintaining a positive attitude; it's about actively using that positivity to drive meaningful change. By combining optimism with concrete actions and leveraging their unique strengths, leaders can significantly impact their communities and foster an environment where positive change is not just possible but achievable.

Choices and Actions Dictate Outcomes

The fact that choice and action dictate outcomes emphasizes a powerful principle: our choices and actions significantly shape the outcomes and experiences of our lives. This concept reminds us of the control and influence we have over our destinies, underscoring the importance of conscious decision-making and intentional action.

It elaborates on how every choice, whether small or significant, sets off a chain of events shaping our future. This perspective shifts the focus from external circumstances to personal agency, suggesting that while we may not have control over every aspect of our lives, our choices and actions are the primary tools to influence our path.

This understanding encourages a sense of empowerment and responsibility. It implies that we are not merely passive recipients of life's happenings; instead, we are active participants who can steer the course of our lives. This realization compels individuals to reflect more deeply on their decisions, considering not just immediate gratification or convenience but the long-term implications of their choices.

Additionally, it underscores the importance of deliberate action. It's not enough to make a choice; translating that choice into action propels us toward our goals and aspirations. These actions become potent catalysts for change and achievement when aligned with our choices and values.

The principle of choice and action dictating outcomes also entails accepting responsibility for the consequences of our decisions. It promotes an attitude of accountability, where individuals recognize their role in shaping their lives and take ownership of their successes and failures.

Choice and action dictate outcomes, which calls us to be mindful and intentional in our decision-making and to follow through with actions that align with our desired outcomes. It recognizes that while we may not control every situation, we can choose our responses and actions, shaping our life's trajectory. This understanding is critical to taking control of our destinies and actively shaping our future.

The Significance of Deliberate Action

Deliberate actions highlight the crucial role of intentional and purposeful actions in achieving our goals and living a life that aligns with our values. This concept stresses the importance of acting and ensures that each action is thoughtfully considered and deliberately chosen to contribute effectively to our desired outcomes.

Deliberate action is about making choices that are not impulsive or reactionary but are deeply rooted in a clear understanding of what we want to achieve and why it's essential. This level of intentionality requires a keen awareness of our values, goals, and the potential impact of our actions. When our actions harmonize with our core values and long-term objectives, they become more meaningful and fulfilling.

Deliberate actions are more likely to be efficient and effective. This efficiency stems from a focused approach where energy and resources are concentrated on tasks that directly contribute to achieving our aims. Deliberate actions help minimize wasted effort on unproductive activities, enhancing overall productivity and satisfaction.

They can lead to more rewarding outcomes. When we intentionally choose actions that align with our goals, we are more invested in the process and the results. This investment increases the likelihood of success and brings a more profound sense of fulfillment and achievement when those goals are realized.

These types of actions also involve a proactive approach to life. Instead of passively responding to circumstances or external pressures, deliberate action means actively shaping our journey. It's about being the author of our own story, taking the initiative to create the life we envision for ourselves.

In addition, deliberate action often requires planning and forethought. It involves setting clear goals, devising strategies, and anticipating potential obstacles. This planning helps us to navigate challenges more effectively and stay on course towards our goals.

The Impact of Action on Authenticity in Personal and Professional Life

The impact of action is a fundamental principle that underscores the importance of taking deliberate steps to manifest one's values and beliefs into tangible outcomes.

In personal and professional life, this concept highlights how authenticity is an internal ethos and a dynamic practice that must be consistently demonstrated through our actions. By acting authentically, we bridge the gap between our inner values and the external world, reinforcing our true selves in every facet of life.

In personal relationships, the authenticity that comes from genuine action can deepen connections and enhance trust. When actions reflect true intentions and feelings, relationships are strengthened and enriched. This is because genuine actions convey respect and a commitment to the relationship, which are critical for building lasting bonds and fostering mutual understanding.

Professionally, the impact of action becomes even more pronounced. Authenticity expressed through consistent and honest actions can transform organizational culture and leadership in the workplace.

When leaders act congruent with their stated values and commitments, they establish credibility and inspire their teams. This can lead to higher levels of engagement, improved morale, and greater productivity. Authentic actions in leadership show employees that they are valued members of the organization, encouraging them to also engage in genuine interactions and contribute their best work.

Furthermore, in a professional setting, the authenticity of action encourages an inclusive environment where diverse ideas and perspectives are valued. When everyone in an organization feels empowered to act authentically, collective creativity and innovation can flourish, leading to better problem-solving and more effective solutions. This inclusivity benefits individual employees and boosts the organization's ability to serve a diverse customer base effectively.

Authentic actions also significantly impact personal development and career advancement. By consistently aligning actions with personal and professional goals, individuals can drive their careers forward in a manner that remains true to their core values. This alignment ensures that career progress does not come at the expense of personal integrity or happiness but enhances overall life satisfaction.

Ultimately, the impact of action in personal and professional life reaffirms that authenticity is active practice. It requires a conscious effort to understand and define one's values and live them out through consistent actions. This dynamic expression of authenticity ensures that our personal and professional lives flourish and genuinely reflect who we are, fostering a sense of fulfillment and purpose that permeates all aspects of our lives.

The Impact of Actions

Your actions are the clearest expression of who you are. While thoughts and intentions matter, it is what you *do* that defines your impact, your character, and your legacy. Authenticity is not a trait reserved for a few; it's a practice. It's about showing up consistently, staying true to your values, and making decisions aligned with your core beliefs even when no one is watching.

Here are ten powerful, practical, and timeless tips to help you stay authentic across all areas of life:

1. Self-Reflection

Self-reflection is the cornerstone of authenticity. It requires making time regularly whether daily, weekly, or monthly to pause and evaluate your actions, intentions, and reactions.

Ask yourself, "Do I behave differently at home than I do at work? Why?"

This exercise can uncover whether you're living according to your values or simply performing for acceptance. The more honest and frequent your self-check-ins, the more aligned your outer life becomes with your inner truth.

Authenticity starts when we hold up the mirror to ourselves, without judgment but with curiosity and grace.

2. Align Actions with Values

Living authentically means your actions are a reflection of your core beliefs, not societal trends or peer pressure. This begins with identifying your values such as honesty, compassion, innovation, or justice and evaluating if your daily behavior supports them.

For instance, if you value kindness but often speak harshly under stress, there's a misalignment. Recognize these gaps and intentionally shift your behavior. Whether it's in personal finances, career choices, or relationships, alignment brings peace, integrity, and fulfillment.

3. Embrace Vulnerability

Vulnerability is often mistaken for weakness, but in truth, it's the doorway to deeper connection. It means having the courage to say "I don't know," to ask for help, or to share your failures. In personal and professional settings, vulnerability humanizes you. It allows others to see your true self and trust your intentions.

When you share your fears or admit a mistake, you create a space for empathy, learning, and mutual respect. Authenticity thrives where vulnerability is welcomed.

4. Cultivate Genuine Connections

Authenticity cannot exist in isolation. True connections are built on shared respect, empathy, and trust. In your personal life, strive to go beyond surface conversations ask meaningful questions and really listen.

In your professional life, take time to understand colleagues' goals and concerns. When you engage with others without hidden agendas or performative politeness, you invite real relationships to develop. The deeper the connection, the easier it is to stay authentic and create environments where others do the same.

5. Communicate Transparently

Transparent communication is essential to authenticity. It means expressing your true thoughts and feelings clearly and respectfully. It involves being direct without being unkind and avoiding gossip or sugar-coating truths to preserve false harmony.

In the workplace, transparent leaders and team members build trust, reduce misunderstandings, and solve problems faster. At home, open dialogue strengthens bonds. Practice active listening, clarify your intentions, and be willing to speak your truth even when it's uncomfortable.

6. Practice Integrity in Leadership

Integrity is walking your talk especially when no one is watching. Authentic leaders are not just respected for their results but admired for their consistency and character.

This means making ethical decisions, admitting when you're wrong, and treating everyone with respect regardless of rank or gain. Integrity in leadership fosters a culture of accountability and openness, where others feel safe to speak up, take risks, and be themselves. It is the foundation of sustainable influence.

7. Embrace Your Uniqueness

Your authenticity is rooted in your individuality. Instead of conforming, celebrate what sets you apart your story, accent, perspective, culture, and experiences. These are your superpowers.

Innovation and creativity flourish in diverse environments where everyone feels free to bring their whole self. Whether you're applying for a job or leading a project, bring your unique lens to the table. Authenticity means showing up as you are, not who you think others want you to be.

8. Be Mindful in Professional Settings

Authenticity doesn't mean oversharing or disregarding professional norms. It means being mindful of how to integrate your true self within your professional role.

Express your ideas clearly, advocate for your values, and respect the cultural context of your workplace. Mindfulness allows you to adapt without pretending and connect without compromising your essence. When authenticity meets professionalism, productivity, creativity, and team morale improve.

9. Assess Your Work Environment

Sometimes, we suppress our authenticity to fit into environments that don't value it. Ask yourself, "Do I feel safe being myself here?" If not, consider whether the environment can change or if it's time to transition.

Your well-being depends on your ability to live in alignment. If your job or team punishes honesty, diversity, or growth, your authenticity will wither.

Choose environments that celebrate, not stifle, who you are.

10. Influence Cultural Change

Being authentic can be a revolutionary act in environments that reward conformity. But your example can be the catalyst for change. Speak up for inclusivity, acknowledge others' contributions, and share your story openly. When people see you thriving as your true self, it gives them permission to do the same. Over time, your influence can reshape a culture, making it safer and more empowering for everyone to show up authentically.

Applying these tips, you can lead a more authentic life that enriches your interactions and professional achievements.

Action-Oriented Leadership

In leadership, action is the driving force behind sustained success and relevance. Leaders across business, education, healthcare, and community service must recognize that stagnation is synonymous with regression in today's dynamic and ever-evolving landscape. The commitment to continuous improvement and innovation is not just a strategy but a necessity for those aiming to lead effectively and make a lasting impact.

Pursuing excellence requires leaders to treat their contributions as work in progress rather than finite achievements. This mindset instills a culture of excellence where the status quo is regularly challenged, and the drive for betterment is constant.

Leaders are tasked with perpetually evaluating and reassessing their approach to service, and asking tough questions about effectiveness, emerging needs, and efficiency are essential to this process. This self-evaluation is critical for pinpointing areas that need improvement and ensuring that services remain relevant and impactful.

Innovation is a pivotal element of continuous improvement. It demands a departure from traditional methods and embraces openness to new ideas and experimental approaches. Leaders should cultivate an environment that encourages creativity and welcomes and explores new ideas that could revolutionize practices. This might mean integrating new technologies, experimenting with novel strategies, or reimagining established procedures.

However, the journey towards continuous improvement and innovation is not meant to be traveled alone. It involves the collective efforts of team members, stakeholders, and clients or beneficiaries. Engaging these groups provides diverse insights and fosters a shared commitment to excellence, making the process a collaborative endeavor that benefits all involved.

Embrace continuous improvement and innovation; leaders ensure their actions lead to effective, relevant, and continually enhanced services to meet the world's changing demands. This commitment helps prevent complacency, propelling leaders and their organizations towards better practices and innovative solutions that stand the test of time.

Future Generation Development through Proactive Leadership

Future generation development underscores the pivotal role that current leaders hold in nurturing and preparing tomorrow's leaders. Effective leadership transcends personal accomplishments, emphasizing the crucial responsibility of fostering the next generation. This responsibility is fundamental for the continuity of leadership and the advancement and sustainability of any society or organization.

Developing future leaders involves more than just the transfer of knowledge and skills. It requires a holistic approach that includes mentoring, providing growth opportunities, and inspiring young leaders to reach their full potential. This comprehensive mentorship and guidance are essential to instill the values, ethics, and vision necessary for effective leadership in the future.

In a rapidly changing world that faces complex challenges, the need for competent, innovative, and adaptive leaders is more crucial than ever. Current leaders are tasked with ensuring that the next generation is equipped with technical skills and knowledge and the critical thinking, creativity, and emotional intelligence required to navigate and lead in an increasingly complex world.

It is also vital to create opportunities for young leaders to practice and hone their skills. This can be achieved by giving them meaningful responsibilities, involving them in decision-making processes, and allowing them to lead initiatives. Such experiences are invaluable in building their confidence, decision-making abilities, and leadership style.

The commitment to developing future leaders reflects a vision that goes beyond the immediate achievements of individual leaders and extends to their impact on fostering a continuous wave of leadership. This ongoing process is crucial for any society's or organization's growth, progress, and long-term success. By investing in the development of future leaders, current leaders not only ensure a legacy of sustained leadership but also contribute to the broader goal of societal advancement and prosperity.

Prescriptions for Purpose: A Call to Action

Imagine waking up every morning with a deep sense of clarity, knowing that your life is not just passing by but is being lived with intention. Too many people exist without truly living, waiting for life to "happen," instead of taking ownership of their purpose.

Purpose is not a luxury reserved for a few; it is a prescription for all. It is not something you stumble upon; it is something you intentionally cultivate. And just like a medical prescription, failing to apply purpose to your life has consequences: regret, stagnation, and unfulfilled potential.

Purpose, however, is not confined to grand gestures or world-changing missions. It is present in the small, consistent ways we invest in ourselves and others. A purposeful life is not dictated by status, wealth, or talent; our daily mindset and habits shape it.

Where do you begin? Right here. Right now. These prescriptions are not mere suggestions but imperatives for living with impact.

1. Invest Time in Self-Discovery

Before purpose can take root, you must know yourself. Who are you beyond titles, responsibilities, and expectations? How do you respond to adversity, success, and uncertainty? What environments and relationships help you thrive? True self-awareness eliminates self-doubt, making you a confident force in your pursuits. Take the time to understand what genuinely brings you joy, what drains you, and what fulfills you. Purpose is only sustainable if it aligns with who you truly are.

2. Set Clear Goals

The purpose without direction is like a ship without a compass. Set specific, measurable, and meaningful goals that guide you toward your desired future. Understand that long-term success is built on a foundation of small, deliberate steps. Each goal should be a stepping stone toward a larger vision, ensuring that every action you take moves you forward.

3. Develop and Execute an Action Plan

A goal without a plan is a mere wish. Identify the steps needed to bring your aspirations to life. Be flexible but committed, adjusting your approach without losing sight of your purpose. Regularly assess your progress, celebrate your wins, and seek guidance when necessary. Success is a result of consistent effort, not occasional bursts of motivation.

4. Cultivate Self-Discipline and Set Non-Negotiable Boundaries

Discipline is the silent architect of greatness. Establish habits that align with your purpose and refuse to compromise on core values such as integrity, trustworthiness, and consistency. Set clear boundaries to protect your time, energy, and focus. A purposeful life requires saying no to distractions and prioritizing what truly matters.

5. Invest in Others

True fulfillment is found in service to others. Make a habit of uplifting and empowering those around you. Be generous with encouragement, patience, and kindness. Your impact is magnified when you help others discover their purpose. Purpose is not just about personal success; it is about collective progress.

6. Seek and Share Knowledge

A purposeful life is one of continuous learning. Knowledge humbles you when received and makes you generous when shared. Be open to learning from diverse perspectives and actively mentor those who can benefit from your experiences. The more you invest in personal and shared growth, the richer your life becomes.

7. Maintain a Healthy Life Balance

The purpose should not come at the expense of overall well-being. Your work, relationships, health, and spirituality must coexist in harmony. Avoid extremes; neglecting one area for the sake of another creates long-term instability. A purposeful life thrives on balance, ensuring no part of you is left behind.

8. Build Resilience and Adaptability

Purpose is not a smooth, straight road; it is a path with obstacles, detours, and moments of doubt. Resilience is the key to enduring setbacks without losing focus. When challenges arise, remind yourself why you started. Adaptability allows you to adjust your approach without abandoning your purpose.

Those who succeed are not necessarily the most talented, but those who refuse to give up.

Final Charge

You now hold the prescription for purposeful living. But a prescription is useless if left unfilled. What will you do with this knowledge?

* ✶ Will you take ownership of your purpose or wait for life to happen to you?

* ✶ Will you make intentional choices or let distractions dictate your path?

* ✶ Will you commit to a life of meaning or settle for mere existence?

The decision is yours. But remember this: A life without purpose is a life wasted.

CONCLUSION

START NOW. START TODAY.

LIVE WITH PURPOSE.

In weaving together, the loops of *Prescriptions for Purpose*, it is understood that life's journey, like the stories shared within these pages, is an ever-evolving tapestry of experiences. From the rugged terrains of hardship to the peaks of achievement, each chapter has served as a guidepost, illuminating the path of growth, resilience, and transformation.

As we navigate the various aspects of personal and professional life, we encounter the undeniable impact of actions on how deliberate choices and earnest efforts carve out the niches where we find success and satisfaction. These stories underline the importance of authenticity, reminding us that the essence of authentic leadership and meaningful relationships lies in being genuine and authentic to ourselves and others.

The lessons drawn from each chapter guide how we might excel as individuals and how we can effectively inspire and prepare future generations. They foster a culture of continuous improvement and innovation, emphasizing that leadership is not about maintaining the status quo but challenging it and aspiring to elevate everyone along with us.

Moreover, the discussions on the significance of authenticity in personal and professional realms reiterate that our interactions are most fruitful and our endeavors most successful when rooted in sincerity and genuine engagement. As we cultivate a persona that aligns with our deepest values, we empower ourselves to live lives of greater purpose and alignment.

This book concludes not with an ending but with an invitation to each reader to take these lessons into the world and apply them. It is a call to action to live intentionally, lead compassionately, and continually strive for a legacy that not only resonates with our aspirations but also ignites the potential in others to do the same.

Embrace *Prescriptions for Purpose* as a toolkit to navigate the complexities of life, leveraging every chapter as a bridge towards a more fulfilling and impactful existence. Herein lies the opportunity to transform every challenge into a victory and every interaction into a chance to learn, grow, and influence.

Let the journey continue, with each step informed by the wisdom encapsulated in these pages, as we strive to make a difference in our lives and the lives of others.

The voyage of existence is not mere survival but about prospering; it's not just about existence but about thriving. And the genesis of it all lies in care. And if we breathe, there is a purpose for being alive. Thank you.

ABOUT THE AUTHOR

D r. Wilfred Njah is a Cameroonian-born physician whose journey from the heart of West Africa to the forefront of American healthcare exemplifies ambition, resilience, and an enduring passion for compassionate service. Raised in a culturally rich household steeped in traditional values and communal responsibility, Dr. Njah's early life was shaped by a deep appreciation for education, integrity, and the transformative power of service. These foundational principles became the guiding compass for his career, propelling him across continents and academic disciplines in pursuit of medical excellence and community impact.

A graduate of The George Washington University School of Medicine and Health Sciences, Dr. Njah's academic path reflects his relentless pursuit of knowledge and service. While earning his doctorate in medicine, he not only mastered the clinical sciences but also developed a keen awareness of the complex social factors influencing patient health.

This understanding inspired him to dedicate his career to addressing healthcare disparities and enhancing service delivery for underserved populations. His medical training, coupled with his early experiences in Africa, instilled in him a unique dual perspective one that bridges traditional community care with evidence-based Western medical practice.

What distinguishes Dr. Njah is not just his clinical expertise but his holistic approach to healthcare leadership. His work as a healthcare consultant extends beyond hospital walls. He is an innovator in designing healing environments that promote both physical and emotional recovery. He champions models of care that address the social determinants of health factors such as housing, income, education, and systemic inequality believing that true healing can only occur when the whole person and their environment are considered.

Beyond medicine, Dr. Njah is a dynamic trainer and mentor in the areas of personal development, leadership, and sales. He is a firm believer that empowerment begins with education and access to opportunity. Through his workshops and mentorship programs, he trains individuals especially those from marginalized backgrounds to recognize their potential, refine their communication skills, and lead with confidence. His teachings are rooted in empathy, real-world experience, and a profound belief in the human capacity to grow and transform.

Dr. Njah's landmark work, *Prescriptions for Purpose: Medicine, Choices, and the Impact of Compassionate Care,* captures the essence of his philosophy. Blending autobiography with professional insight, the book reflects his life's journey, the lessons learned through hardship, and the unwavering commitment to helping others live and lead with purpose. It is both a personal narrative and a blueprint for others in the medical field to embrace their roles as healers, leaders, and agents of change.

His international experience also includes public health initiatives, including his role as Director of Health Equity for the Kids of Tomorrow Foundation, a nonprofit organization working in rural Nigeria to provide accessible healthcare and education. Dr. Njah has been instrumental in building clinics, securing medical donations, and coordinating cross-cultural medical missions. His advocacy for global health equity reflects a deep understanding of the structural barriers to care and a visionary mindset focused on long-term, sustainable solutions.

Currently residing in Boston, Massachusetts, Dr. Njah remains a passionate advocate for health education, professional mentorship, and financial empowerment. His impact resonates through his work with young professionals, emerging leaders, and patients alike. He continues to consult, teach, and speak globally on topics ranging from leadership in healthcare to culturally competent care delivery and legacy-driven career development.

Dr. Njah embodies what it means to live with intention. Whether he is working one-on-one with patients, leading public health projects, or mentoring future medical leaders, his mission remains the same: to heal, to serve, and to inspire. His life and work stand as a testament to what is possible when purpose and profession unite.

To learn more about Dr. Wilfred Njah, his programs, and his mission, visit: www.wilfrednjah.com.

www.ingramcontent.com/pod-product-compliance
Lightning Source LLC
Chambersburg PA
CBHW031428270326
41930CB00007B/618